Who the Hell is B.F. Skinner?

Who the Hell is B.F. Skinner?

And what are his theories all about?

Tom Buxton-Cope

First published in Great Britain in 2020 by
Bowden & Brazil Ltd
Felixstowe, Suffolk, UK.

ISBN 978-1-9999492-8-0

To find out more about other books and authors in this series,
visit www.whothehellis.co.uk

Contents

Introduction

There are few in the history of psychology as unique and polarizing as B.F. Skinner. For his critics, he is the man who tried to reduce the complexity and wonder of the human mind to the mechanistic level of the rats and pigeons pressing levers and pecking keys for food pellets in his laboratory. They argue that, in proposing we are all merely products of our environment, he was stripping individuals of their autonomy, free society of its freedom, and humans of their humanity. They also felt his new school of psychological thinking – radical behaviourism – posed a clear threat to the cherished cultural traditions and humanistic values of twentieth-century America, and therefore his ideas had to be resisted. For others, however, he was the ground-breaking scientist who had achieved the most predictable and trustworthy results ever seen in psychology. In doing so, his science of behaviour helped shift psychology away from speculative attempts at uncovering hidden mysteries of the mind, towards a true science of behaviour, with the potential to raise the profile of psychology to that of the natural sciences. Far from posing a threat to society, Skinner was attempting to ensure its survival by challenging the status quo with his case for a new cultural design, based on scientific understanding rather than historical accident.

Whichever view you take, no one can deny Skinner's bold willingness to ask difficult questions and to find practical solutions to real-world problems. Not only was he a psychologist and social philosopher, but he was an inventor too, and he regularly combined his range of talents and interests in pursuit of such solutions. He tried his hand at creating everything from apparatus to improve the care of babies, through to pigeon-guided missiles that could be used by the military in wartime; his ingenuity knew no bounds. Even as a novelist, Skinner was problem-solving. The fictional 'utopian' society depicted in his book, *Walden Two* (1948), enabled Skinner to describe a way of life that was independent of political action and in which waste and consumption were drastically reduced. In what would later become a bestseller, he had laid out a possible strategy for designing a culture in which human conflict and our environmental impact were both greatly minimized. The sheer variety of his daring and intriguing work saw him appear on the cover of *Time* magazine in 1971 which only served to increase the public attention he received.

It is hard to say why Skinner's ideas touched a nerve for so many people. Was it symptomatic of the political sensitivities that existed in post-war American society? Or are there certain enduring core beliefs, held by so many, with which his ideas will always jar? Whatever the reason, Skinner certainly evoked a reaction in people: he was hanged in effigy by university students, he was thoroughly investigated by the FBI, and vice president Spiro Agnew (1969 to 1973) publicly warned Americans against him. It is hard to believe then that, despite arousing such animosity, Skinner was also the man who was awarded no less than 18 honorary degrees, named Humanist of the Year, and given the National Medal of Science by President Lyndon Johnston (1963 to 69). To have been both vilified and celebrated to such an astonishing degree demonstrates not just the divisiveness of Skinner's work, but also its longevity. Although Skinner's work spanned most of the twentieth century, through different social and political landscapes, its legacy will be felt for much longer. To this day, his theories of conditioning and reinforcement are unrivalled in their breadth of application to everyday settings, from schools and workplaces, to prisons and psychiatric units.

Who the Hell is B.F. Skinner? considers where and how such an original figure in psychology lived, and who influenced his radical new approach to understanding human behaviour. He was not the first to call himself a behaviourist, so it is vital to understand what it was about his specific contributions, and the world in which they were made, that made his ideas and the application of those ideas in the real-world so controversial. In exploring his psychological, practical, and philosophical approach, we might begin to question whether we, as humans, are who we think we are, and what significance these questions might have in the rapidly changing environments of the modern world.

1. Skinner's Life Story

Burrhus Frederic Skinner was born on 20 March 1904, in the small town of Susquehanna, Pennsylvania, USA, close to the New York State border. The young Skinner was known as 'Fred' to his family and friends, possibly because he always found his first name, which was his mother's maiden name, 'troublesome' as it always needed to be spelled out and explained. Growing up, Fred lived in a home environment he described as 'warm and stable' together with his parents and his younger brother, Edward, known as 'Ebbie'. His father, William Skinner, had come from relatively poor beginnings and succeeded in gaining local prominence as a lawyer. His mother, Grace Burrhus, was a talented singer who had attended the same school as William, Susquehanna High School, graduating with excellent grades. William's marriage to Grace in 1902 helped to cement his growing reputation as a family man with excellent career prospects, and the couple could look forward to raising their children in what was a prosperous time in America. The nation was emerging as a world power after the economic depression and the Spanish–American War of the 1890s, entering the new century with the promise of huge progress in technological innovation. The Skinners' life in the railroad town of Susquehanna in many ways reflected the general feeling of prosperity in America at the time. William was to become district attorney, president of the Susquehanna Board of Trade and a speaker at political rallies in support of the Republican Party. When Fred was born, the *Susquehanna Transcript* declared that 'Susquehanna has a new law firm, "William A. Skinner & Son"', a prediction that William greatly enjoyed sharing with his friends and associates (Bjork, 1997).

Two-and-a-half years later, in 1906, Ebbie was born. The boys grew up in a household in which there were clear expectations and a strict code of behaviour enforced by their mother, Grace Skinner. She was regularly heard asking 'what will people think?' in response to any behaviour she felt fell short of her expectations. The importance both William and Grace placed on their standing in the community and being seen to behave correctly undoubtedly had a great influence on Fred and may explain the sense of inadequacy and embarrassment he went on to feel in a variety of social situations. Grace's tendency to criticize rather than praise Fred as a child may also have influenced some of his later psychological theories emphasizing the effectiveness of reward and reinforcement over punishment in shaping behaviour.

In Fred's eyes, however, his parents' strict code was not always applied in equal measure to both of the boys, Ebbie clearly being the favourite. Fred later recalled a number of rule-breaking acts by his brother – such as finding William's revolver and accidentally shooting a hole through a bureau – going unpunished by his parents. The revolver incident is something Fred believed he would certainly have been punished for. Ebbie was a fun-loving and affable boy with an interest in sports and a social ease that

Fred lacked. He was, in all likelihood, more easily controlled than Fred, whom his parents found eccentric and difficult, which may explain the leniency his parents showed towards Ebbie with regard to their social code. Far from Fred being jealous of his brother, however, he was very fond of him, and the two of them played together a great deal in their earlier years.

Fred, the Inventor

For everyone who lived in Susquehanna, daily life was paced by the coming and going of the trains passing through the town, and the huge railroad 'shops' (repair factories). Susquehanna only existed because the Eerie Railroad had come to the area in the 1840s and it soon had the largest and most complete shops for railroad repairs in America, employing large numbers of the towns' citizens. The Eerie Railroad was the main artery of the town and the train timetable became its heartbeat, regulating the rhythm of life for its shop workers and everyone else alike. Loud blasts of the factories' 'shop whistle' at key times throughout the day would dictate the start and end of work, but also when the town's stores opened and closed, and when meals were served and eaten. Fred had always been fascinated by his boyhood environment, with its railroad and the machinery of its repair shops. It seems likely that the way in which the shop whistle triggered responses in the citizens of the town helped shape Skinner's future experiments in radical behaviourism.

His interest in fixing and building was evident in much of the play he engaged in with his brother when they were children. Outside of their square two-storey wooden house, Fred would go on to reflect that his 'yard was a mess, the town was a mess, the surrounding countryside was largely primeval' (Skinner in Bjork, 1997). However, far from seeing this chaos as a barrier, Fred saw it as an opportunity to learn 'to explore, to organize, to select, to construct without a plan'.

Fred's experimenting knew no limits. He built roller-skate scooters, rafts, seesaws, water pistols and 'a steam cannon with which [he] could shoot plugs of potato and carrot over the houses of [their] neighbors'. He even described trying 'again and again to make a glider in which [he] might fly' (Skinner in Dews, 1970). His propensity for inventing on such a prolific scale demonstrated a bold willingness to solve the problems posed by all aspects of the world around him. In childhood, he approached problems in much the same way that he would approach scientific research as an adult: learning through improvization and through trial-and-error rather than any deliberate, premeditated process. His production line of inventions also showed he could match ambition with the hard work and perseverance required to see these ideas though to fruition; another hallmark of his later scientific work. Fred would spend hours crafting, shaping, cutting, sticking, making and remaking his various contraptions, admittedly some more successfully than others.

Fred, the Entrepreneur

As a young boy, as well as regularly playing with his brother, he also spent a lot of time with his best friend, Raphael Miller, whom he called 'Doc' because his father was a doctor. Doc and Fred both shared an interest in gadgets and contraptions. They once set up a telegraph line between their houses to send messages to each other, although the messages were frequently so confusing that they often ended up calling each other on the telephone to find out what they were both trying to say. During one childhood summer, Doc and Fred attempted to make one of their inventions pay. Exploring the environment close to home, they had found out that when they tried to pick ripe elderberries, the unripe ones came off the branches too. To address this, they built a device that was able to separate them out. The devicc was a trough made from a bent piece of metal which they could pour water down and into a bucket. When the berries were introduced, they found that the ripe ones would sink into the bucket while the unripe ones would be pushed over the edge to be thrown away. They soon decided to use their efficient sorting device to gather large numbers of ripe elderberries before selling them door-to-door. This early experience in business was, in many ways, a first glimpse of the way Frcd combined his entrepreneurial spirit with his inventiveness, much as he did as an adult.

Fred, the Intellectual

As well as being a keen explorer of the outside world, using his various devices and contraptions, Fred was also a keen explorer of ideas and stories, and from an early age he would spend a great deal of time reading and writing at home. When he was around 10 years old, Fred built himself a box using a packing case in which he could read and write, free from the distractions of family life. There is nothing particularly unique about a young boy building a den in which to hide from others, but Fred's den was not made simply for hiding. His inventiveness would not permit it. Fred's box-like den could be closed off with a curtain and, inside, he had built shelves to hold his writing materials and reading books, and positioned a candle for working in the dark. His creation was in many ways the first 'Skinner Box' (see Chapter 3), and was not only symbolic of the invention that would lead to his famous discovery years later at Harvard University, but also representative of his desire to make time and space to think.

Growing up, it became increasingly clear that Fred was not like either of his parents. Although William had achieved a great deal in becoming a lawyer from his humble beginnings, he had also struggled to achieve many of his lofty ambitions, running unsuccessfully for mayor shortly before Fred was born. Perhaps most disappointing of all, William had struggled to form a bond with his eldest son. Fred considered his father to be socially inadequate and also hinted that his political and intellectual shortcomings were the reason for his inability to climb the professional ladder any further than he already had. Fred's view of his mother was not much better. Despite sharing a love of music with her, Fred clashed with Grace, due to her controlling nature. From an early age, he felt that neither his parents nor his brother shared his intellectual interests or ability. It wasn't until he started at Susquehanna public school that he was able to form a relationship that could truly begin to satisfy these intellectual needs.

Although Fred did well in all subjects at school, one teacher was influential beyond any other. Mary Graves, his Art and English teacher while at school, inspired Fred well beyond the specific concerns of her particular subject specialisms. While his parents found his intellectual curiosity and ability to think independently unconventional and difficult, Miss Graves championed these traits. She encouraged him to find answers for himself through his own independent enquiry and detailed note-taking – skills that became hallmarks of his scientific work as an adult. As a school pupil however, Fred's main love at school was not science, but creative writing – a passion for which Miss Graves had no doubt helped instil in him.

Fig. 1 Miss Graves

Hamilton College

On graduating from high school, it was on the recommendation of a family friend that Skinner decided to apply to study at Hamilton College in Clinton, New York, where he was duly accepted to study English Literature. Despite being the first of his family to attend college, he nonetheless arrived feeling confident that he would excel in his new environment, free from the shackles of parental control and small-town concerns.

He initially found the transition to life as a freshman challenging, with his speech teacher objecting to his sentence construction and pronunciation of certain words which, for a man prone to social embarrassment, was a humiliating experience. This served as an instant reminder for Skinner that, although he had left the small-town environment of his upbringing behind, its influence was still very much a part of him, as was his mother's concern with 'what people might think'. He struggled to make friends in his first year at Hamilton, with his classmates being generally more interested in sports and the fraternity social calendar. Ebbie may well have found it much easier to fit in at Hamilton than his brother, but for Fred Skinner it was an isolating experience, leaving him feeling detached and disillusioned.

Events got much worse, however, during Fred's first spring break spent at the family home in Scranton, where they had moved shortly before he had begun at Hamilton. Ebbie had emerged from the bathroom complaining of an excruciating headache and asked for a doctor before fainting. As the doctor arrived, Fred rushed to get his parents from the church service they were attending. Ebbie died before they returned home, at the age of just 16. A physician later concluded that he had died from a massive cerebral haemorrhage. His loss was devastating for the Skinners. Nonetheless, Fred would later reflect on the way in which he had been able to watch his brother dying with remarkable detachment. Observing his parents reaction to the news, too, he recalled feeling moved by their grief and yet somehow detached and separate from it. Fred was not an unemotional person and yet he was capable of viewing events of such personal and emotional magnitude with a level of dispassionate objectivity that would be impossible for most people.

Fig. 2 Skinner, aged 19

Over the next three years at Hamilton, Skinner threw himself into writing, producing stories and poems, some of which were published in *The Hamilton Literary Magazine*. He made a best friend in John 'Hutch' Hutchens whom he had met in his second year, and together they helped write and edit one of the Hamilton campus publications, the *Royal Gaboon*. After graduating, Fred planned to spend one year living back with his parents with the aim of writing a novel.

The Dark Year

Skinner embarked on his year of writing with a sense of purpose by building himself a suitable place to work at home. He fashioned a work table, bookcase, and a rack that could be positioned on a chair to hold books while he read: another box-like working environment, just as he had built as a 10-year-old. What he lacked though was an idea around which to formulate the novel he so craved to write. Despite his best efforts, his entire output from the period he went on to call his 'dark year' consisted of a dozen short newspaper articles and a few models of sailing ships that he had built.

Perhaps another reason why he called this period his dark year was because this was also the time during which his Grandfather Burrhus fell ill and died, with Fred at his bedside. Although this affected him a great deal, he was able to witness his grandfather's passing in an extremely detached and objective manner, just as he had done with Ebbie. Following his grandfather's death, he went on to remark in his diary that 'except for certain reflex muscular activities the minute before and minute after [death] were alike' (Skinner in Bjork, 1997). In many ways, these descriptions mirror the objective, accurate writing style that were to become characteristic of B.F. Skinner, the behavioural psychologist.

Later in his dark year, Fred escaped to New York City for a few months where he worked as a bookstore clerk. It was while working there that he first happened upon books by Ivan Pavlov and John B. Watson, two behavioural scientists who had a major influence on his later work. He found their ideas impressive and exciting and it left him keen to learn more.

The soul-searching triggered by his experiences during the dark year had led Skinner to the field of psychology; a field he had previously known little about and yet one which he would come to realize encapsulated many of his early interests. In his autobiography, Skinner later remarked that his father, 'possibly because he never quite understood how to get on with people, was always watching them', frequently drawing young Fred's attention to their behaviour. As an aspiring writer and avid reader of literature, Skinner realized the stories he had always read and tried to write were invariably psychological in nature. As a young inventor, entrepreneur, and intellect, Fred had wanted to test devices and behaviours in order to understand the world around him, and in the science of psychology, all of these skills and interests could finally be combined and developed.

Psychological Beginnings

At the age of 24, Skinner enrolled in the Psychology Department of Harvard University. As an independent thinker, keen to experiment and develop original ideas, and with little time for ideas that he considered to be unintelligent, Skinner was fortunate at Harvard to find a mentor with a similar outlook. William Crozier was the chair of a new department of Physiology. Crozier's scientific approach was to study the behaviour of 'the animal as a whole' without trying to deduce, as the psychologists did, the internal workings of the mind. This was precisely the approach that appealed most to Skinner, having been convinced from reading the work of behaviourists like Pavlov and Watson. Crozier gave Skinner time and space to experiment and, with his inventiveness and talent for building new equipment, Skinner did exactly that.

Working with laboratory rats, he constructed one new piece of apparatus after another, responding each time to suggestions made by the rats' behaviour. This eventually led to him creating a rectangular box containing a lever which, if pressed by the rat, would trigger the delivery of a food pellet down a chute to be eaten by the rat. This invention, and other variations of it, would eventually become known as the 'Skinner Box'. As he continued to develop his apparatus, and after a few lucky accidents, Skinner also invented a mechanical device called a 'cumulative recorder' that could accurately record the rats' rate of lever-pressing. Together, these inventions helped Skinner to make his breakthrough scientific finding. Skinner was able to spend the next five years at Harvard developing and refining these ideas further as part of a series of experiments which would go on to appear in his first book, *The Behavior of Organisms* (1938). This experimental and theoretical work is explained in detail in Chapter 3.

Marriage and Children

In his final year at Harvard, Skinner was introduced by a friend to Yvonne 'Eve' Blue who was visiting. They were instantly attracted to one another; Yvonne finding Skinner handsome, articulate and, as a Junior Fellow at Harvard, someone with excellent prospects, while Skinner found Yvonne charming, attractive, and someone who shared many of his literary interests. Having recently accepted a teaching position at the University of

Fig. 3 Skinner with Yvonne

Minnesota, Skinner would later confess that he wanted to marry Yvonne, not only due to their compatibility but also because he felt he would need emotional support after leaving Harvard. They married on 1 November 1936. Yvonne found the early years of their marriage difficult with their social lives revolving around other couples in Skinner's new department. However, despite her misgivings about her new life in Minneapolis and the lack of career opportunities it afforded her, she bravely persevered and settled into the role of wife and mother, giving birth to the Skinners' first child, Julie, in 1938, and Deborah in 1944.

Despite both sharing a love for literature and a devotion to their two daughters, the relationship between Yvonne and Fred Skinner in many ways mirrored that of Fred's parents. Not only did both relationships lack any true happiness but also, like his father before him, Fred required a great deal of emotional support from his wife. Both men were accused of extreme egotism yet both had quite fragile egos and never felt that their wives gave them sufficient support or encouragement in their respective careers. As Fred later remarked, 'I think Eve envied my success and didn't have one of her own', presumably referring to the fact that Yvonne had never been afforded the opportunity to develop her own career (Skinner in Bjork, 1997).

Project Work

In the early 1940s, during the height of World War II, Skinner was keen to use his skills and experience to help in the war effort. He sought funding for a project to train pigeons (which by this time had replaced rats as his laboratory test subject of choice) to guide missiles towards their enemy target. His idea was met with a great deal of resistance at first but he did go on to receive national military funding to begin the top-secret work on pigeon-guided missiles which became known as 'Project Pigeon'. Despite having some success, however, the programme was eventually cancelled in 1944.

Fresh from the disappointment of Project Pigeon, Skinner was about to begin work on a very different project. While Yvonne was pregnant with their second child, she had wondered whether Fred might be able to use his aptitude for inventing solutions to problems to design a crib for their baby. Skinner soon began work on his version of a 'baby tender' (or crib) that would eventually become known as the 'aircrib'. After finalizing his design, Skinner then invested a great deal of time in trying to launch his invention commercially but, despite initial interest from various parties, his efforts were ultimately in vein.

The work that took place during Project Pigeon and the aircrib project are described in full in Chapter 4 along with other examples of Skinner's wide-ranging applications of his ideas.

Walden Two

Following the end of the war, Fred accepted a position as chairman of the Psychology Department at Indiana University in Bloomington, a town that Yvonne greatly disliked, and which only added to their marital difficulties. The post was from 1946–7 and as Skinner's ideas were beginning to grow in influence, the Society of the Experimental Analysis of Behavior was formed, meeting for the first time in Indiana. This emerging field of study, inspired by Skinner's pioneering work while at Harvard, had taken a number of years to get to this point and its gradual rise to prominence would continue over the years ahead.

It was while in Indiana that Skinner also produced one of his most important pieces of writing. This piece of writing, however, was not like his others. It was not even psychological, at least in the scientific sense. It was a work of fiction called *Walden Two*. The title of the book is a direct reference to Henry D. Thoreau's book, *Walden* (1854). Thoreau's book details his experiences while living alone for two years in a woodland cabin near Walden Pond and in which he feels able to acquire all of the necessities of life by living simply in the natural surroundings. Skinner's Walden Two community is described as having the benefits of living in a place like Thoreau's Walden, but 'with company'. It is, as the book says, 'Walden for two' – meaning a place for living well, but within a thriving, planned community, rather than in solitude. It had been inspired, at least in part, by a dinner party conversation towards the end of the war in which a friend had commented on her son and other young people returning home and to the old ways of doing things. Challenged to suggest what he would have them do instead, Skinner began work on a novel which would explore a vision of an alternative community called Walden Two.

The book follows a soldier who has recently returned from the war as he invites friends and his former psychology professor, Professor Burris, to visit the community which consists of about

1,000 members. They meet the designer of the community, Frazier, who explains how the happy and hard-working community members have had their behaviour carefully shaped using behavioural techniques. Skinner was well aware of the similarity between the name of Burris and his own name, Burrhus, and even suggested that Frazier may have been a blend between his nickname, Fred, and Crozier, his scientific mentor at Harvard. He later wrote: 'I did not know until I had finished the book that I was both Burris and Frazier' (Skinner, 1976). The book is discussed in more detail in Chapter 5 as part of an exploration of Skinner's wider philosophical perspective – radical behaviourism.

After publication, *Walden Two* received both praise and criticism in equal measure. Concerned at some of the negative reactions, Skinner tried to get hold of his old friend, Hutch, for advice, by this time a senior review editor for *The New York Times*. However, much of the criticism aimed at the book did not concern its style or story so much as its message. It was viewed by many as a political manifesto, advocating the scientific control of society. Indeed, Skinner did go on to consider the feasibility of a real Walden Two.

Although interest in the novel was modest at first, over time it would soar. Only 9,000 copies of the book were sold from its publication in 1948 up to 1960, but by the early 1970s, sales had reached 100,000, prompting national debate over the issues it raised. By the time Skinner died in 1990, total sales were close to 2,500,000.

Talking, Teaching and Technology

The reason for the delayed surge in interest in *Walden Two*, as well as Skinnerian Psychology more generally, owes much to another of Skinner's inventions. Unlike his earlier projects, which were plagued by scepticism and doubt, his invention in the field of education gained much more widespread positive attention.

Towards the end of his time in Indiana, Skinner accepted an invitation from Harvard University to give the William James Lectures in 1947. This was soon followed by an invitation to rejoin the Psychology Department there in 1948, bringing Skinner and his family back to Cambridge, Massachusetts. The following year, during the summer of 1949, Yvonne temporarily left Fred and the children, staying for a short period in New York City. While this was an extremely unsettling time for the Skinners, Yvonne's brief departure was perhaps not entirely unexpected. Fred spent a lot of time working away from home and, as he later admitted, had engaged in 'sexual experimentation' while the family were living in Indiana (Skinner in Bjork, 1997). The fact that he argued these affairs had little positive or negative effect on his marriage suggests an emotional detachment from the relationship – something he had shown towards other loved ones at key moments in his life. While he does seem to have been concerned about his wife, his dedication to his endeavours at university and elsewhere clearly took precedence. In his work, he saw himself as dutiful (Skinner, 1983) and, notwithstanding this period of sexual affairs, it seems that he took the same approach towards his marriage in quite a literal sense. There was clearly a lack of engagement between Fred and Yvonne beyond the basic marital duties. The lack of interest he showed in his wife seems to have been reciprocated to an extent by Yvonne when she suggested in a 1971 interview with *Cosmopolitan* magazine that Fred didn't talk to her much about his work '... because one, I'm not a psychologist and wouldn't understand, and two, I'm not terribly interested'. While Skinner may not have succeeded in achieving a meaningful connection through his marriage, it had given him the security of a long-term relationship and the joy of two daughters.

Back at Harvard, Skinner taught a course for undergraduates, the material he produced for the course forming the basis of his book, *Science and Human Behavior* (1953). Throughout the 1950s, Skinner worked with a large number of exceptional graduate students, the work produced in this period resulting in *Schedules of Reinforcement* published in 1957. In the same year, Skinner also managed to finish a book that he had been writing, on and off, for 20 years. The book, *Verbal Behavior* (1957), set out to apply Skinner's theories on learning and reinforcement to language acquisition and development. He dedicated the book to his daughters who he referred to as his primary sources for the book. While they were undoubtedly influential – he and Yvonne had both recorded and analyzed a great deal of their early language – language had been an interest to Skinner right from his childhood. His passion for reading was evident in Miss Graves' class at school and had led him to study English at Hamilton College and even to attempt to become a writer during his dark year. Literature was also one of the great passions that he shared with Yvonne. She was an avid reader and frequently introduced him to new novels. The two of them would even read Trollope aloud to each other. However, in attempting to explain human language, Skinner was tackling an aspect of human behaviour that had for a long time been considered too complex for his animal-derived theories to explain. Skinner's attempt to do just that in *Verbal Behavior* is summarized in Chapter 4.

Perhaps one of the reasons *Verbal Behavior* had taken so long to write (aside from the complexity of the subject matter), was that he had written much of the book while simultaneously developing another of his inventions. Just as was the case with his aircrib project, here again it was his daughters who served as the inspiration behind this latest venture. More specifically, his inspiration had come from a chance encounter with the mainstream school system after he was invited to visit Deborah's school for a day. Observing one teacher try to cater for the needs of a classroom full of children, it struck him that this approach simply could not meet the individual needs of all of the students in the class who would inevitably find the teacher was moving either too fast or too slow for them. Given his interest in drawing on his scientific work to invent practical solutions, Skinner soon became involved in developing a teaching machine. The basic idea was that each child would have such a machine which would allow them to make progress at their own pace, and in doing so, learning would be personalized according to each individual's needs.

Skinner would spend the next 10 years developing teaching machines and related techniques for use in the classroom. The work he did during this time contributed to his next book, *The Technology of Teaching* (1968) which he dedicated to the teacher who had exerted such a huge influence on him: Miss Graves. His work on teaching machines and the related idea of programmed instruction are discussed more fully in Chapter 4.

The Rise to Media Prominence

B.F. Skinner would remain at Harvard for the rest of his life. In 1968, President Lyndon B. Johnson awarded him the National

Medal of Science and a year later he published another of his comprehensive works, *Contingencies of Reinforcement* (1969). However, it was the release of his next book two years later, called *Beyond Freedom and Dignity* (1971), which prompted a huge surge in media attention. In this book Skinner brought together many of the philosophical ideas he had written about throughout his career as a radical behaviourist. This included his position that people's entrenched belief in free will and individual autonomy was preventing human beings from using science to build happier and more effective societies (see Chapter 5). Skinner soon reached the height of his public exposure and found himself embroiled in controversy, resulting in a series of television appearances as well as him appearing on the cover of *Time* magazine that same year. His ideas provoked a condemnatory reaction, with his critics ranging from psychotherapist Carl Rogers to Vice President, Spiro Agnew. Agnew publicly warned Americans against him, using an address in Chicago to argue that Skinner's 'behavioral thinking [is] very dangerous, and it is completely at odds with our basic belief in the dignity and worth of the individual' (Rutherford, 2009).

While Skinner undoubtedly had many strong critics, he had many supporters too, with *Beyond Freedom and Dignity* stirring a national debate. In the same year that his effigy was hanged at Indiana University, he was also named 'Humanist of the Year'. Perhaps this polarization of opinion was, at least to an extent, a sign of the times in America at the height of the Vietnam War. While Skinner was a critic of the war, many interpreted his position as advocacy of totalitarianism. A Freedom of Information Act would later reveal that the FBI had kept a file on Skinner, who was reportedly quite aware that the FBI had monitored his activities. Both the government's cold-war anti-communist sentiment and the esteem in which Skinner was held by his colleagues are reflected in the heavily censored pages contained in the file. Skinner felt that much of his newly found public notoriety had ultimately stemmed from misrepresentations of his work. It was out of a desire to correct what he saw as inaccurate portrayals of his work in the media that Skinner wrote *About Behaviorism* in 1974.

Final Years

Even after his retirement in 1974, Skinner remained professionally active. A prolific writer all of his life, Skinner continued to write professional articles in retirement as well as completing his three-volume autobiography. His timer would ring at 5 a.m. every morning to wake him and he would make his way down his basement staircase to his rectangular-shaped study, where he would work at his writing desk on papers and articles until the timer sounded again at 7 a.m. His box-like working environment echoes the ones created in his earlier life: at home writing during his dark year, and even in the packing-case den he had created as a child. Furthermore, his rigid adherence to the sound of his timer echoes the shop whistle of his childhood in Susquehanna. He was certainly a creature of habit, or perhaps – like the rat pressing levers for food – he was simply an organism that had been continuously reinforced to behave in this manner. Either way, his behaviour would not change, even after being diagnosed with Leukaemia in 1989. The following year, aged 86, he presented his final paper to a crowded auditorium of 20,000 psychologists from around the world at the American Psychological Association in Boston, where he received their Lifetime Achievement Award. Shortly before the convention he told the Associated Press, 'I'm writing a paper which is my summing up of what psychology is all about and attacking cognitive psychologists [...] The cognitive psychologists won't like it, but that doesn't bother me at all. I will be dead in a few months' (*Los Angeles Times*, 1990). B.F. Skinner died on 18 August 1990.

B. F. Skinner 's Timeline

Skinner

- **1904** Burrhus Frederic Skinner is born
- **1906** Younger brother, Edward Skinner, is born
- **1922** Begins study at Hamilton College; Edward Skinner dies
- **1928** Enrols in the Psychology Department of Harvard University
- **1936** Marries Yvonne Blue; Begins teaching at Minnesota University
- **1938** Publishes ***The Behavior of Organisms***; Julie Skinner is born
- **1944** Project Pigeon; Deborah Skinner is born
- **1945** Begins as Chairman of the Psychology Department at Indiana University
- **1948** Publishes ***Walden Two***; Returns to teach at Harvard University

World Events

- **1904** Ivan Pavlov wins the Nobel prize for his studies of conditioning
- **1905** Edward Thorndike publishes ***The Law of Effect***
- **1913** John B. Watson publishes **'Psychology as the Behaviorist Views It'**
- **1914** Outbreak of World War I
- **1920** Watson and Rayner conduct the Little Albert experiment
- **1927** Pavlov publishes ***Conditioned Reflexes***
- **1928** Watson and Rayner publish ***Psychological Care of Infant and Child***
- **1936** Ivan Pavlov dies
- **1939** World War II begins
- **1945** World War II ends
- **1947** Cold War begins

1953 Publishes ***Science and Human Behavior***; Builds teaching machine prototype

1953 Crick and Watson discover the helical structure of DNA

1958 John B. Watson dies

1959 Noam Chomsky publishes his critique of BF Skinner's ***Verbal Behavior***

1968 Publishes ***The Technology of Teaching***

1969 Publishes ***Contingencies of Reinforcement***

1971 Publishes ***Beyond Freedom and Dignity***

1971 Skinner features on the cover of ***Time*** magazine; Vice President Agnew publically warns Americans against Skinner

1973 The end of direct US involvement in the Vietnam War

1974 Publishes ***About Behaviorism***; Retires

1989 Diagnosed with Leukaemia

1990 Wins Lifetime Achievement Award from the American Psychology Association; BF Skinner dies

2. Influences on Skinner's Thinking

B.F. Skinner was not the first behavioural psychologist. Well before he had begun his first experiments at Harvard University, the psychological school of behaviourism had already established a tradition of radical thinking. Ivan Pavlov (1849–1936), Edward L. Thorndike (1874–1949), and John B. Watson (1878–1958) were three psychologists who challenged and changed the whole field of psychology beyond recognition, and Skinner's work owed a great deal to their research. To suggest, however, that Skinner's behaviourism was simply a continuation of their work would be to overlook the originality of the theories Skinner would go on to produce.

Watson's Behaviourist Manifesto

Although there is some debate over the precise moment when behaviourism began, many would point to 1913, when Skinner was only a child, and to a lecture given at Columbia University by John Broadus Watson, a man whom Skinner would go on to read about and be influenced by as an adult. Titled 'Psychology as the Behaviorist Views it', or 'The Behaviourist Manifesto' as it is sometimes referred to, Watson argued for a drastic revision of the aims and methodology of psychology. According to him, psychology should become 'an experimental branch of natural science', focused on the study, prediction and control of behaviour.

Published as an article in the *Psychological Review* later that year, Watson's address proposed a radical change of direction for a field which, until then, had been focused primarily on what Watson would refer to as 'mentalism' – the study of internal mental processes such as consciousness, perception and thought. The dominant approaches to psychology up until this point had revolved around, firstly, introspection, pioneered in the 1870s by Wilhelm Wundt, who many regard as one of the 'fathers' of psychology (along with William James), and secondly, psychoanalysis, pioneered by Sigmund Freud in the late 19th century. Wundt's introspection involved the training of participants to systematically report on their own mental processes in response to a range of different stimuli (the word introspection literally meaning 'to look inwards'). Freud's psychoanalytic approach, meanwhile, had shifted the focus towards unconscious mental processing, rather than conscious thinking alone. Regardless of whether they were studying conscious or unconscious processes though, to Watson, both of these approaches were simply pursuing different versions of mentalism. These approaches may have had their differences but, to Watson, they both ultimately involved subjectively speculating on hidden processes which could not be directly observed by the researcher and therefore could not be objectively checked or validated in any way. Watson was convinced that 'the mind' could not be studied in a scientific way, and that past attempts to do so by Wundt, Freud, and others, had only served to hinder the advancement of psychology.

Watson's manifesto would argue that psychology, in the new era, should no longer be considered the science of the mind and, instead, that it should focus on the externally visible behaviour of the individual. This would go on to be seen as a paradigm shift in psychology – a scientific revolution whereby the dominant aims, assumptions, and methodology of the day were being challenged and replaced by new ones. The behaviourist approach was so-called because it considered behaviour to be the unique parameter by which human activity could be objectively tested and understood, independent of consciousness or the concerns of mentalism.

Watson's approach would not limit itself to human behaviour, however. For him, behaviourism must also include animals who he equated with humans as both were seen to follow the same behavioural scheme. Even if human activity has become more complex and elaborate over time, it is nonetheless seen to be derived from the same fundamental laws that govern all animal activity. This can be seen clearly in the work that Skinner would go on to do, studying lever-pressing behaviours in rats and target-pecking behaviours in pigeons, amongst other things. These ideas were also evident well before Watson's famous lecture in 1913 though, with Ivan Pavlov's research into salivation in dogs often cited as another key contribution to the birth of behaviourism.

Pavlov, the Honorary Psychologist

It is interesting that Pavlov's research is seen to have played such an important role in behavioural psychology's rise to prominence, not least because Pavlov himself was not a psychologist. Pavlov was a Russian physiologist who spent the large part of his

Fig. 4 Ivan Pavlov

career studying digestion in dogs. He would never have imagined that, in the decades to come, he would go on to be listed as 24th on a list of the most influential psychologists of the twentieth century, with B.F. Skinner – one of the people he influenced so much – appearing in first place (Haggbloom et al, 2002).

Pavlov's classic research findings came about during work he was conducting into salivation in dogs. In order to collect and measure their saliva more precisely, he managed to successfully externalize a salivary gland. While measuring their salivation in response to food under different conditions, he noticed that the dogs tended to start salivating even before any food was actually delivered to their mouths. Pavlov quickly became fascinated with what appeared to be the dogs' instinctive response to the sight of the technician who normally fed them. He called this phenomenon, 'psychic secretion', and set about seeing if he could demonstrate this in a more controlled and reliable way.

In order to determine whether the dogs' psychic secretion (salivation caused by expectation of food) could be triggered by a specific external stimuli, Pavlov designed an experiment in which he would sound a buzzer shortly before giving the dogs food. He discovered that once the buzzer had been sounded a few times before feeding, the sound of the buzzer alone would be enough to cause the dogs to salivate. He called this a 'conditional reflex' but this process of learning through association would go on to become more widely known as 'classical conditioning'. The process can be described in terms of stimulus and response as it is all based on a response (reflexive reaction) to a stimulus (object or event) which does not have to be learned – such as a dog's salivation at the sight of meat. This unlearned response is called an 'unconditioned response' and the stimulus which elicits that response is called an 'unconditioned stimulus'. In the case of Pavlov's dogs, salivation is the unconditioned response to the unconditioned stimulus of food because dogs do not need to learn (or be conditioned) to salivate in response to food; the behaviour occurs instinctively.

Classical conditioning builds on an unconditioned stimulus–response behaviour such as this by pairing the unconditioned stimulus (e.g. meat) with a neutral stimulus (a stimulus to which an animal does not have an instinctive response – such as a buzzer). In the classic account of Pavlov's dog research, the buzzer acted as the neutral stimulus because a buzzer does not naturally cause the dog to salivate or respond in any other clearly defined manner. During the process of conditioning, the neutral stimulus must be consistently presented alongside the unconditioned stimulus in order for the two stimuli to become associated (i.e. sounding the buzzer immediately before presenting the food on several occasions). The key discovery from Pavlov was to show that this process of learning by association, once firmly conditioned, was sufficient for the once-neutral stimulus (e.g. the buzzer) to produce the response (salivation) even in the absence of the unconditioned stimulus (food). The neutral stimulus had therefore become a 'conditioned stimulus' producing a now 'conditioned response' of salivation as this stimulus–response behaviour needed to be learned; the behavioural response to that stimulus does not occur instinctively.

Pavlov also showed that this learned association is not permanent. If food stopped being delivered after the bell had sounded, while the dogs would initially continue to salivate when they heard the bell, this association would eventually begin to diminish and disappear, through a process known as 'extinction'. These pioneering findings would go on to help Pavlov win the Nobel Prize in 1904, the year Skinner was born.

Although Pavlov had achieved recognition for his work before Watson's 'Behaviourist Manifesto', and well before Skinner had made his first contributions to the field, his work only really gained mainstream attention in the West through the writings of Watson.

The 'Little Albert' Experiment

On first hearing about Pavlov's dogs and the process of classical conditioning, it is not always immediately obvious what the implications of his work were beyond dogs salivating in response to the sound of a buzzer. Watson, however, was convinced that this process of learning could help to explain a number of other poorly understood behaviours, not just in animals but in humans as well. In 1920, together with a graduate student, Rosalie Rayner, Watson set about demonstrating how classical conditioning could be used to explain the formation of a mental illness in humans.

In what has become an infamous study in the history of psychology, known as much for its unethical nature as it is for its ground-breaking findings, Watson and Rayner recruited a healthy nine-month-old boy referred to as 'Albert', with the aim of conditioning him to develop a phobia. Using procedures similar to those used by Pavlov, Watson wanted to show how a stimulus of which a human child has no instinctive fear (a neutral stimulus) could be paired with a stimulus which is instinctively feared (such as the loud banging of metal bars and frightening masks, experienced in close proximity) in order to produce a phobic response.

In the classic account of the 'Little Albert' experiment, Albert is first presented with a white rat to demonstrate that children do not instinctively fear animals like rats, and sure enough Albert showed no fear – he played with the rats. The rats were initially a neutral stimulus, producing no response, as expected. Watson then set about trying to scare Albert by banging two metal bars together to make a loud noise close behind him, which would make him scared and cry. This crying was clearly an unconditioned response to the unconditioned stimulus of the loud noise. In order to then condition a phobia, Watson and Rayner would present Albert with the white rat while also making the loud noise (pairing the rat and the noise). After making him cry in this way several times, they tested whether Albert had formed an association between rats and crying by presenting him with the rat once more but without banging the metal bars together. Just as Pavlov's dogs had salivated in response to the sound of a bell on its own, Albert began to cry at the presentation of the rat, even in the absence of any noise. What was once a neutral stimulus (the rat) had now become a conditioned stimulus producing the conditioned response of fear; Albert had learned to have a phobia of rats.

In further experiments, Little Albert seemed to generalize his fear response beyond merely white rats. He reportedly went on to show distress at the sight of several other furry objects, such as a rabbit, a dog, a seal-skin coat, and even a Santa Claus mask with a white, cotton beard (Schwartz, 1986). Watson and Rayner's original plan was to follow up on their conditioning of a phobia in Albert by using a similar process to condition a calm response to rats in him once more. In the end though, Watson had no time to attempt such desensitization with Albert, and it is thought likely that the infant's fear of furry things stayed with him for life.

Despite the unethical nature of Watson and Rayner's experiment, it had served to demonstrate one of the many ways that classical conditioning may help to explain behaviours in humans. It had done so through observing externally visible behaviours and without the need for any form of mentalism. Although Watson did not manage to use behaviourist techniques to treat and desensitize Albert, these ideas would go on to form the basis of an effective treatment for phobias called systematic desensitization which continues to be used to this day. This kind of application of behaviourist principles to solve real-world problems would become a hallmark of Skinner's later work too.

Watson's Later Years

Despite the scientific success of the Little Albert experiment in 1920, Watson's career was soon to suffer following revelations of his affair with his student, Rosalie Rayner, whom he had worked with on the project. His wife, Mary Watson, soon filed for divorce and both the affair and divorce proceedings became front-page news in the Baltimore newspapers, leading John Hopkins University to ask Watson to leave his faculty position. Watson and Rayner did go on to marry and have two children who they raised according to behaviourist principles.

After resigning from John Hopkins University, Watson's influence in the field of psychology diminished and he began working in advertising for the J. Walter Thompson Agency (transforming the power of advertising through the introduction of behaviourist principles). Although Watson did continue to write and publish influential material, the man who had played such an important role in the birth of behaviourism was in some ways, by this point, already on the path to being superseded by Skinner, who was soon to rise to prominence at Harvard. One of the works Watson published during this time produced one of his most famous behaviourist quotes. In his 1925 book, *Behaviorism*, Watson wrote:

> *'Give me a dozen healthy infants, well-formed, and my own specified world to bring them up in and I'll guarantee to take any one at random and train him to become any type of specialist I might select—doctor, lawyer, artist, merchant-chief and, yes, even beggar-man and thief, regardless of his talents, penchants, tendencies, abilities, vocations, and race of his ancestors.'*

This is Watson's most cited quote, probably because it sounds so radical but also so simple. In it, he clearly situates the behaviourist position as being firmly on the nurture side of the nature–nurture debate. What is often left out of this quote, however, is the last line in which he acknowledges the exaggerated nature of the statement by saying: 'I am going beyond my facts and I admit it, but so have the advocates of the contrary and they have been doing it for many thousands of years.'

This final sentence clearly shows that Watson's position was not quite as radical as the previous statement had suggested, acknowledging that behaviourism did not have all of the answers yet. Watson would stop writing for popular audiences in 1936, following the death of his wife, Rayner, the previous year. By this time, Skinner had announced himself as the new face of behaviourism, but the work of Watson and Pavlov had undoubtedly played a key role in getting him to that point.

Skinner's Literary Influences

Skinner's initial interest in psychology was sparked long before he had come across the work of Pavlov and Watson. Although there were a number of signs during Skinner's early life of the talents and interests he would go on to demonstrate as a psychologist, his interest in psychological science was only truly sparked during the time he called his 'dark year'. This period actually amounted to more like 18 months in the time immediately following his graduation from Hamilton College, and was a time when Skinner, struggling to launch his desired writing career, had spent a great deal of time searching for inspiration by reading widely. It is likely that he first read about Watson in the August 1926 issue of *The Dial*; a magazine of the time that published original fiction and poetry, critical articles and reviews. One review included in that issue was written by British philosopher, Bertrand Russell, who had made a favourable reference to Watson. Russell, more than any other writer, was responsible for introducing Skinner to the philosophy of behaviourism (Bjork, 1997). Russell's positive remarks towards Watson in his review illustrated the sensitivity shown by editors of *The Dial* to the role of science in the post-World War I era. Many critics had attacked science in the wake of the war, holding it responsible for the mechanized slaughter of millions that had taken place. Russell, however, argued that, if used with intelligence, science had the power to benefit all of humanity. These kinds of sentiments would be reiterated by Skinner in many of his later published works.

Although Skinner's dark year saw him move away from wanting to write fiction towards working in science, fiction did also play a role in this shift. On the recommendation of his friend and mentor from Hamilton College, Percy Saunders (a college dean and chemistry professor), Skinner read a number of books that reinforced his growing desire to be part of the scientific revolution that had been earlier heralded by Watson. H.G. Wells's *The World of William Clissold* (1926) gave him a glimpse of society being rearranged along scientific lines which may have inspired his thinking on the benefits of deliberate cultural design. H.G. Wells may have influenced Skinner too, through an article published in the *New York Times* magazine in which he stated that he would choose to save the man of science, Ivan Pavlov, over the man of literature, George Bernard Shaw, if he had but one life-saver.

Towards the end of his dark year, Skinner made the decision to apply to study Psychology at Harvard University, partly on the advice of Saunders, whose brother taught Physics there. Following the decision, he quickly moved to New York's Greenwich Village in February 1928. It was here, while working as a part-time book clerk on Fifth Avenue, that he first read Watson's *Psychological Care of Infant and Child* (1928). His growing interest in psychology was only reinforced by the cultural trend in the Village at the time, amongst writers and intellectuals, to discuss Freud and psychoanalysis at parties.

The Harvard Years

In September 1928, Skinner commenced his studies at Harvard University. One of the courses he enrolled in was a Physiology course run by William Crozier (1892–1955). Unbeknownst to Skinner at the time, Crozier was to become a key influence on his development as a psychologist. Often described as having a no-nonsense and even aggressive professorial style, Crozier expected his students to have the confidence and determination to follow their own experimental interests, and Skinner was greatly impressed. Crozier specialized in tropism – the response of a whole organism to an external stimulus. This was a field Skinner had already read much about at Hamilton in *The Organism as a Whole* (1916) by Jacques Loeb, a German-born American physiologist whom Crozier had studied under.

Despite Crozier being mainly focused on the movement of lower organisms, he did also work with rats. This focus on the behaviour of rats as an entire organism (as opposed to focusing on the surgical isolation of glands, as was the case for Pavlov) became a key part of Skinner's early work at Harvard. Despite Crozier's approach to study playing a key role in Skinner's early work with rats and despite his aggressive style, Skinner went on to remark that Crozier also gave him the time, space and encouragement he needed to conduct his own research. Crozier, like Skinner, enjoyed working with his hands as much as his mind, experimenting with new devices and inventions to observe how organisms (such as rats) would respond to different stimuli.

Thorndike's Puzzle Boxes

During this early period at Harvard, Skinner was undoubtedly also influenced by the work of Edward Lee Thorndike (1874–1949). Thorndike had introduced 'puzzle boxes' many years earlier (around 1898) to test animal intelligence. These were boxes in which an animal, such as a cat, could be placed where they would have to try to escape in order to access food. Each box had a door that could be opened by pressing a bar or pulling a lever inside the box. Thorndike measured the length of time it would take the animal to escape from the box over a number of trials. He was testing ideas that had earlier been proposed by George Romanes (1848–1894) in his book, *Animal Intelligence* (1892), in which he had stated that animals, like humans, think things through when dealing with a new environment. However, Thorndike found that, rather than thinking through their escape from the puzzle box first, the cats would instead move around in a trial-and-error manner and would only discover the importance of the bar or lever by accident. Following their accidental discovery, the cats would know what to do when placed in the box again, becoming progressively faster at escaping on subsequent trials. By plotting each cat's escape time against the trial number, Thorndike was able to produce the first known animal learning curves, very similar to the ones Skinner would go on to produce when measuring a slightly different aspect of rats' behaviour.

Based on his puzzle-box findings, Thorndike argued that, rather than proactively thinking a situation through before behaving (as Romanes had suggested), animals will instead physically interact with their environment using trial-and-error until a successful result is obtained to which they then respond accordingly. These ideas led Thorndike to proposing the 'law of effect' which was, in many ways, the precursor to Skinner's theory of operant conditioning (outlined in Chapter 3). The law of effect suggested that responses that produce either a satisfying effect, or a discomforting effect, in a particular situation are more likely to occur again in that same situation.

While Thorndike's puzzle-box methodology and law of effect may appear extremely similar to the Skinner box and Skinner's theory of operant conditioning, there were some key differences. Methodologically speaking, while both men used box-like apparatus to test animals and produce learning curves, the animals, apparatus, and measurements were different and, crucially, Skinner's more advanced apparatus enabled him to produce far more reliable learning curves. Theoretically speaking, while both men emphasized the importance of behaviour being rewarded, Thorndike did not deny the existence of consciousness and used the language of mentalism when referring to a 'satisfying' effect, something which did not sit well with Skinner's focus on observable behaviour. Thorndike was also a proponent of eugenics – the idea that some people possess a superior genetic make-up to others and that ways of ensuring those genes become more common in the human gene pool would be advantageous to society. While Thorndike's work may have been influential to many aspects of Skinner's later work at Harvard, their perspectives differed greatly, and Skinner would go on to clearly distinguish himself from his behavioural predecessors.

Fig. 5 Skinner with his friend, Keller, 1931

The influence of Thorndike may have occurred primarily through another of Skinner's Harvard professors, Walter Samuel Hunter (1889–1954). Hunter developed Thorndike's work with puzzle boxes further by devising more sophisticated 'puzzles'. For example, he exposed different animals (including rats) to multiple-choice chambers in which the animals had to learn to exit a chamber in which a light bulb had been lit. The animals were detained before being allowed to choose the correct door as part of a demonstration of delayed-response learning. Hunter used his findings to show that behaviour was more complex than Thorndike had assumed and Skinner would follow Hunter's lead in his future career by building increasingly more elaborate variations on his basic procedure.

The Turning Point

During his first year at Harvard, Skinner became best friends with psychology graduate student, Fred S. Keller (1899–1996). They shared similar views on psychology, despite having quite different tastes in music, sports and women. Skinner later described Keller as being the philosopher of behaviourism while he himself was the practitioner of science. Keller helped convince Skinner that it didn't matter that he didn't believe in the concept of 'studying the mind' and that he could still get his doctorate in psychology by making a science out of the study of behaviour. Skinner would later dedicate his book, *Science and Human Behavior*, to Keller.

It was in 1930, after abandoning the study of squirrels for rats and after hours of inventing and tinkering with equipment in his laboratory in response to the rats' behaviour, that Skinner made his ground-breaking discovery (covered in detail in Chapter 3). The learning curves produced by the rats in his 'Skinner Box' were remarkably smooth and predictable and Skinner recalls Crozier being extremely excited by his findings. Although Skinner would not complete his full account of what he would call 'operant conditioning' until the publication of *The Behavior of Organisms* in 1938, he had nonetheless reached a turning point in his career.

Skinner, like Pavlov before him, would continue to talk about stimulus and response until 1935, and only started using the term 'operant' in 1937 as he distinguished his theory of operant conditioning from the classical conditioning of Pavlov and Watson more and more. In defining operant conditioning as learning through reinforcement, however, he did admit to borrowing the term 'reinforcement' from Pavlov. Nonetheless, whereas Pavlov had described conditioning based on physiological reflex responses such as salivation, Skinner focused on conditioning through reinforcement of a *behaviour*. He argued that his operant conditioning was a second form of conditioning to add to Pavlov's classical conditioning (or 'respondent conditioning' as Skinner called it), and that it may help to explain more complex behaviours like thinking where the physiological reflex-based respondent conditioning had failed.

Despite Skinner's claims to have broken new ground, *The Behavior of Organisms* received a great deal of negative reviews at the time. It has been suggested that this arose partly because Skinner had not explained the relationship between his work and that of his behavioural predecessors, such as Pavlov and Watson. Skinner had felt that his approach was new and therefore had no significant relationship with the work that had gone on before. He did receive some encouragement from a number of other sources though, with his friend Keller – who was by then teaching at Colombia University – incorporating the book into his lectures. Another source of encouragement came from another behaviourist, Clark. L. Hull (1884–1952) who, despite having some differences of opinion with Skinner on how behaviourist science should be conducted, nonetheless invited Skinner to speak to his graduate students in New Haven. Hull is believed to be the first, at this time, to refer to Skinner's operant conditioning chamber as the Skinner Box.

Personal and Cultural Influences

Perhaps one of the key reasons why Skinner's early work didn't receive the recognition that it might have deserved, is that it did not impress upon the reader the full implications and possible applications of the ideas it had described. Skinner did later remark that a purely descriptive science is never popular. In the years after 1938, however, Skinner worked hard to explain and demonstrate the fundamental importance, as he saw it, of his radical new form of behavioural science and the ways it should be used to shape and improve all aspects of society. The applications of his work that he went on to develop though were largely shaped by personal and cultural events of the time.

After his marriage to Yvonne in 1936 and the birth of their first daughter Julie, it was the impending birth of their second child, Deborah, in 1943, which had led Yvonne and Fred Skinner to discuss ways he could use his skills and ideas to develop a new baby crib to improve the environment for a new-born infant and its caregiver alike. The following year, the events of World War II inspired Skinner's work to train pigeons to guide bombs as part of Project Pigeon. The next book he was to publish, however, was his novel, *Walden Two*, which was reportedly influenced by his consideration of the world soldiers would return to after the war and the opportunity this gave to design a new way of living by the principles of behaviourism. Perhaps the most attention-grabbing application of his work, though, came in the form of his teaching machines, which were again inspired by one of his daughters as he sat at the back of Deborah's mathematics class on Father's Day in 1953. He also dedicated his book, *Verbal Behavior*, covering language acquisition and development, to his daughters, citing them as his 'primary sources' for the book. Skinner's baby crib (or aircrib, as it would become known), Project Pigeon, and teaching machines are all discussed fully in Chapter 4.

Skinner's Critics

It may come as no surprise that throughout his career, an academic as unique and radical as Skinner was heavily criticized by others who did not share his scientific perspective or worldview. Many of these criticisms, however, acted as a catalyst for Skinner in influencing the future direction of his work. For example, it is thought that it was after being challenged by Alfred North Whitehead (1861–1947), during a casual discussion while at

Harvard, to provide an account of a randomly provided example of verbal behaviour that led Skinner to begin formulating the theories he would go on to present 20 years later in *Verbal Behavior*. Interestingly, Noam Chomsky's (1928–) highly critical review of *Verbal Behavior* is often credited as playing a key role in the cognitive approach gaining prominence around this time. There has, nonetheless, been a resurgence of interest in Skinner's theory of language development more recently.

It certainly took Skinner a number of years to gain the status he enjoyed towards the end of his career. This was, perhaps, the result of others not appreciating the significance of his work or his style of writing. However, the cool reception received for many his early published works and many of his inventions only served to spur him on further to lay out his position with increasing clarity. His 1971 book, *Beyond Freedom and Dignity*, in many ways represents the crystallization of his broader philosophical perspective.

A Pioneer Until the End

While it is clear to see the influence of Pavlov, Watson, Thorndike and others on Skinner's scientific and philosophical work, he went to great lengths to explain the originality of his ideas as well as the power of these ideas to explain and improve all aspects of life. He remained passionate about his own unique form of behavioural science until his dying day, even as mainstream psychology shifted through cognitive and biological revolutions. Although many found his outright rejection of free will dehumanizing, he maintained that this was a truth backed by empirical evidence, and that it had the ability to change humankind for the better.

To this end, he was unwavering in his pioneering mission to convince the world of the need to embrace the facts as he saw them if we are to meet the challenges of the future.

3. Operant Conditioning

The idea that formed the focus of Skinner's early work in psychology, and that went on to help shape much of his subsequent experimental and theoretical work, is that of operant conditioning. In simple terms, operant conditioning can be defined as the process of learning through reinforcement. Whereas Pavlov and Watson had focused on conditioning (the process of learning or acquiring new behaviours in response to environmental stimuli), Skinner would go on to describe an entirely different process through which we learn from the environment.

The problem with classical conditioning (outlined fully in the previous chapter), as Skinner saw it, was that it was entirely dependent upon explaining all behaviour in terms of associations formed between a new (neutral) stimulus and a stimulus to which there was a pre-existing response. For example, Pavlov's dogs only learned to salivate in response to a buzzer (the neutral stimulus) because they had learned to associate the buzzer with the presentation of food to which dogs had a pre-existing, reflex response of salivating. Skinner was unconvinced by the argument that all new behaviour is ultimately based on pre-existing responses or prior learning in this way. He felt classical conditioning (or 'respondent behaviour', as he would often call it) was far too simplistic to be a complete explanation of complex human behaviour. Observing the behaviour of his laboratory rats at Harvard, he was convinced that a huge amount of the behaviours that the rats showed was in no way related to prior events or pre-existing responses, and that instead, much of their behaviour was simply spontaneous.

The idea of 'spontaneity' had not been addressed by Pavlov or Watson in their work, perhaps because it may be seen to imply that organisms like humans have free will and can choose how to behave, free from the governing laws of science and nature. Skinner, however, believed that spontaneity played a bigger part in classical conditioning than had previously been imagined. He began by drawing a comparison between the role that might be played by apparently spontaneous behaviours and that played by genetic mutation in Darwin's evolutionary theory of natural selection. According to the laws of natural selection (and the 'survival of the fittest'), a wide variety of genetic mutations occur across members of a given species. Those mutations which aid the survival of the individual are then 'selected by the environment', ensuring that, over time, they become more common in members of that species in future generations. Applying similar ideas to the behaviour of an organism such as a rat within the lifetime of that individual, Skinner proposed that a range of apparently spontaneous behaviours may be 'emitted' by the organism (rat), unrelated to any prior events in the environment, and that those behaviours which have positive consequences (such as enabling the rat to eat, reproduce, or avoid danger) will be more likely to be repeated while those which have negative consequences will diminish. In this sense, there is a survival of the *fittest behaviours* within the lifetime of each organism rather than a survival of the fittest genes over generations. Skinner called these behaviours, which are unrelated to any prior event, 'operants', and the process by which these behaviours (which lead to desirable consequences) are more likely to be repeated as 'reinforcement'. Whereas Pavlov and Watson had seen behaviour as being under the control of prior (earlier) events, Skinner was proposing behaviour may actually be under the control of posterior (later) events.

In his first book, *The Behavior of Organisms*, Skinner sought to make the distinction between operant and classical conditioning clear from the outset, saying:

> *'The kind of behavior that is correlated with specific eliciting stimuli may be called respondent behavior and a given correlation respondent. The term is intended to carry the sense of a relation to a prior event. Such behavior as is not under this kind of control I shall call operant and any specific example an operant. The term refers to a posterior event, to be noted shortly.'*

Breakthrough Research

The scientific breakthrough that inspired Skinner to develop this idea came as a direct result of the hours he had spent in the laboratory at Harvard inventing new apparatus to record specific animal behaviours. This work ultimately led to two key inventions: the lever box (which went on to become widely known as the Skinner Box) and the cumulative recorder. The design of the box was simple; if a hungry rat placed inside pressed the lever, a food

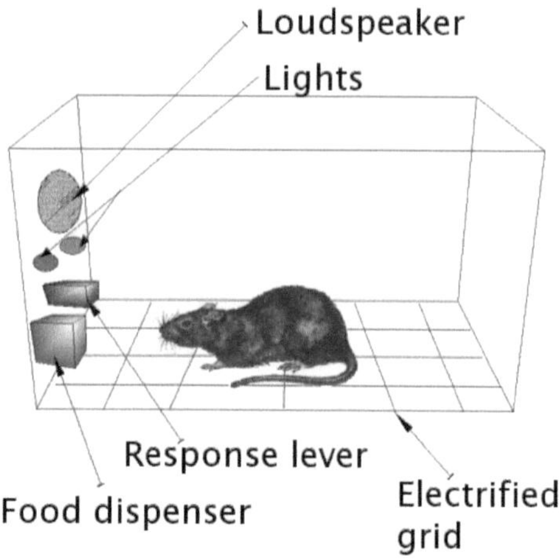

Fig. 6 Skinner Box

pellet would be delivered to the rat via a glass tube. However, in order to realize this, the rat would first need to press the lever and it could take a while for this to happen as the rat explores the new environment until the desired operant behaviour of lever-pressing is shown. Once they eventually emit the desired operant behaviour and press the lever, the food pellet delivered would then act as a 'reinforcer' (a consequence that increases the chances that a specific behaviour will be repeated). The cumulative recorder, meanwhile, was a device that would automatically make a pen-and-ink record of each lever-press on a sheet of paper that gradually unrolled over a cylinder. Over a period of time, this record would form a curve to represent the rate at which the rat pressed the lever; the higher the frequency of the lever pressing, the steeper the curve produced. This measurement is called a 'response rate' and it essentially showed how hard the rat was working.

Using this apparatus, Skinner was able to record remarkably smooth curves; the response rate of the rats became more and more frequent over time as their lever-pressing behaviour was reinforced by the delivery of food. Under such controlled conditions, the same behaviours could be precisely repeated again and again enabling Skinner to develop the principle of operant conditioning that could then be used to accurately predict the future behaviour of the rat.

Extinction and Reconditioning

In the same way that reinforcing a hungry rat's behaviour using food pellets increased the rate of lever-pressing in a highly predictable manner, Skinner also found that this process could be reversed by halting the delivery of food pellets. The rats' lever-pressing would diminish in a similarly predictable way. This loss of a previously conditioned behaviour is referred to as 'extinction' and the rate at which lever-pressing 'dies out' is called an 'extinction rate'. Unlike his breakthrough discovery with response rates caused by reinforcement, however, his discovery of the extinction rate occurred by accident rather than by design, after the pellet dispenser in his Skinner Box jammed while he was away from the laboratory. Nonetheless, when he returned to his equipment he found that the cumulative recorder had produced an equally smooth curve in the opposite direction to that shown when the rat's behaviour was initially reinforced. The term 'extinction' had been used earlier by Pavlov to describe the diminishing salivation by his dogs in response to a buzzer when it has not been paired with food for a number of trials. If we consider how Skinner's form of extinction might work in relation to the everyday lives of humans, it would be interesting to find out how long people would continue to work if their employer stopped paying them their monthly salary. How long would they work in the *hope* that they might be paid, before realizing that they were working for no reward?

Exploring these ideas further, Skinner was able to demonstrate that, after bringing the lever-pressing behaviour to a stop, the operant could be 'reconditioned' at the will of the experimenter simply by dispensing food pellets again. Furthermore, by adjusting the point at which the rats were reconditioned, he found that, here too, he could produce reliable effects on the rats' response rates. For example, the rats could be reconditioned before the lever-pressing behaviour had been fully extinguished. If a second reconditioning closely followed the first, he found that the remainder of the first curve would appear to sum with the second, meaning the second curve would start from a higher point than the first. By regularly starting reconditioning before full extinction has taken place in this way, Skinner showed that successive curves would continue to sum until eventually a complete fusion takes place where the strength of the behaviour would remain at a constant value as long as the periodic reconditioning is maintained. This gave Skinner his first insight into how different patterns of reinforcement would each produce different patterns of behaviour in the rats; something he would study in much greater detail later on in his career through his work on schedules of reinforcement.

Skinner's breakthrough findings were some of the most trustworthy ever produced in psychology and they had been achieved through Skinner's invention and innovation (as well as a slice of luck). However, by focusing initially on reinforcement that was positive (delivering food to a hungry rat), Skinner had only considered one possible consequence (or posterior event) that might follow an operant behaviour. It wasn't long before he began demonstrating the effects that other possible consequences might have on behaviour as well.

Types of Reinforcement

In terms of reinforcement, Skinner acknowledged that two types existed: positive and negative. Positive reinforcement occurs when a behaviour is followed by the addition of something pleasant. For example, when rats and pigeons are conditioned using Skinner's preferred method of dispensing food pellets (which they enjoy) or when a child is praised in a classroom for a correct response to a question. Negative reinforcement, on the other hand, occurs when a behaviour is followed by the removal of something unpleasant. This may be equally rewarding in the sense that we are relieved that the negative experience has stopped. For example, putting on a coat in bad weather is reinforcing as it removes the unpleasant experience of getting cold or wet.

A later adaptation of the Skinner Box incorporated an electrified grid in the floor which, when turned on, would cause the rats to feel an uncomfortable electric current through their feet. In this situation, pressing the lever would turn off the electric current. Hence the rats were negatively reinforced to press the lever to avoid the unpleasant electric current. Both positive and negative reinforcement result in similar outcomes: they both strengthen behaviour by increasing the chances of that behaviour being repeated in future. The difference between the two types of reinforcement is if they strengthen behaviour via the application of something positive (positive reinforcement) or the removal or avoidance of something negative (negative reinforcement).

The Role of Punishment

As well as the two types of reinforcement, another possible consequence of an operant behaviour is punishment, and Skinner did dedicate time to considering its role in conditioning behaviour too. Like reinforcement, Skinner proposed that punishment can occur in one of two ways, also referred to as positive and negative. Positive punishment occurs when a behaviour is followed by the addition of something negative (being told off by a teacher for talking in class) while negative punishment occurs when a behaviour is followed by the removal of something positive (being prevented from going out with your friends). Both types of punishment weaken behaviour by decreasing the chances of it being repeated in future, they simply differ on the way this outcome is achieved.

Skinner dedicated a chapter of *Science and Human Behavior* to punishment, and here he questioned the wide-scale use of punishment in society – notably in our justice, education, and financial systems, to name a few. Skinner made the case for the use of reinforcement instead of punishment to increase desirable behaviour and decrease undesirable behaviour, saying, 'In the long run, punishment, unlike reinforcement, works to the disadvantage of both the punished organism and the punishing agency.'

Skinner did not believe that punishment could be as helpful as reinforcement in modifying behaviour. Not only did punishment cause a negative emotional response in both the punished individual and the one punishing them, but it was also less effective at guiding them towards a desired behaviour. While reinforcement had the power to tell an individual specifically what to do, all that punishment could do was tell them what not to do. Furthermore, Skinner would go on to demonstrate that reinforcement could be used to guide behaviour with a striking level of precision depending on the exact ways behaviour is reinforced.

Schedules of Reinforcement

Working with Charles Ferster (1922–81) at Harvard in the mid-1950s, Skinner wanted to build on some of the earlier work he had done with rats, by investigating the effects of implementing different patterns of reinforcement on the speed of both learning and extinction. They called these patterns 'schedules of reinforcement' and the book they published of the same name in 1957 was an extensive analysis of the various ways in which reinforcements could be arranged over time, together with the impact these schedules had on the response rate and extinction rate in pigeons. By this time in Skinner's career, pigeons had replaced rats as his test subject of choice, with the operant behaviour of pecking a coloured disc replacing the lever-pressing he had originally used when working with rats. The most notable schedules of reinforcement studied by Skinner were continuous, interval, and ratio schedules.

Fig. 7 Example of operant conditioning using a pigeon as the test subject.

Fixed and Variable Intervals

Continuous Reinforcement (or CRF) occurs when the subject (pigeon) receives a reinforcer (food pellet) every time a specific action is performed (disc-pecking). This schedule was shown to produce a fast rate of learning because it quickly establishes a reliable link between the target behaviour and the reinforcer. However, CRF was also found to have an extremely fast extinction rate, as the behaviour would die out very quickly after the food pellets were halted. Applying these ideas to the real-world, this might suggest that treating a dog every time it sits on command may help in the initial training of the new behaviour, but if you simply halt the treats in the belief the behaviour has been learned, the dog may not sit on command for much longer.

These same ideas may be true of human learning and may suggest that once a behaviour has been initially learned, it may be more effective to adopt a different schedule of reinforcement in order to maintain that behaviour over time. In the dog training example, once CRF has conditioned the dog to reliably sit on command, rather than simply halting the treats altogether straight away, the trainer may begin to only treat the dog every now and then. This move away from CRF should make the dog less likely to 'notice' if a treat is not given at any point and therefore the incentive to keep sitting on command will persist for far longer even when the treats are eventually no longer given. The main alternative schedules to CRF are interval and ratio schedules but both these can be arranged in either a fixed manner (set and unchanging) or in a variable manner (varied and changing).

Interval schedules of reinforcement are based on the period of time (or interval) between each reinforcement, and this period of time can be either fixed or variable. A Fixed Interval (FI) schedule involves the presentation of reinforcements at a fixed period of time, provided that the appropriate response has been made. For example, food pellets can be delivered every 30 seconds, provided the pigeon has pecked the disc in the interim period. This schedule yields a response rate that is low just after reinforcement and becomes rapid just before the next reinforcement is scheduled to occur. In other words, the pigeon will learn to not peck the disc immediately after it has received a food pellet but to start pecking the disc more frequently as it nears the end of the 30 second interval. The response rate of an FI schedule may be more moderate than with CRF as reinforcers are not delivered as readily, but the extinction rate is also more moderate (slower to die out) as greater patience is required when intervals are placed between reinforcers.

Fixed Intervals in Application

An example of an FI schedule in humans might be a salesperson making an increased volume of sales calls as the end of the month gets closer in order to hit their monthly sales target. Here, the increased number of sales calls is the response and hitting the monthly sales target acts as the reinforcement.

One interesting observation to arise from Skinner's work on FI schedules with pigeons was that some birds were seen to develop 'superstitions'. When food was dispensed every 20 seconds, regardless of the behaviour of the pigeon, Skinner reported that the behaviour exhibited immediately beforehand became reinforced. For example, if the pigeon coincidentally turned anti-clockwise or made a pendulum movement of its head before the food was dispensed, it could soon be seen consistently repeating that particular movement over and over again in ritualistic fashion. Skinner went on to publish *Superstition in the Pigeon* in 1948 and suggested human superstitions may develop in a similar manner. For example, if on two or three occasions a child performs well on a test having used a particular pen, despite this pen having no real effect on their chances of passing, the child may have been reinforced to do all tests in future with their 'lucky pen'. Likewise, your sports team doing well when you are wearing a particular scarf or shirt may reinforce the wearing of that 'lucky scarf' or 'lucky shirt'. Stimuli may acquire 'unlucky' properties in a similar manner if the person incorrectly connects a behaviour (such as treading on a crack in the pavement) with an unpleasant event that follows (missing your bus) even though these events are not in any way connected.

Variable Intervals and Applications

As well as FI schedules, the other type of interval schedule is called a Variable Interval (VI) schedule. This involves reinforcing behaviour after random (varied and unpredictable) periods of time following the last reinforcement (provided the appropriate response has been made), rather than a fixed period of time. For example, the pigeon might be reinforced after 6 seconds at first, before having to wait 13 seconds, followed by a 3 second interval, followed by an 18 second interval, all provided they have pecked the disc in the random interim period. The unpredictability of this schedule was shown to yield a fast response rate (as the pigeons cannot be sure if a reinforcer will be delivered after a very short space of time) and a slow extinction rate (as the pigeons could equally not be sure whether they were simply waiting for a reinforcer to be delivered after a long period of time). An example of a VI schedule in humans might be a self-employed sales person who cannot be sure when they will next be paid: they may be rewarded quickly for working hard in the short-term but may also be rewarded for working hard over the longer-term and so are incentivized to not give up.

Reinforcing with Ratio Schedules

Moving away from interval schedules, an entirely different schedule of reinforcement would be a ratio schedule. Rather than being based on time intervals, ratio schedules are based on the number of responses (or behaviours) required in order to be reinforced. A Fixed Ratio (FR) schedule involves reinforcement occurring after a fixed (predictable) number of responses has been made. For example, a pigeon may receive a reinforcer (food pellet) after five responses (disc pecks) have been made. Skinner showed that this yielded a fast response rate (as the pigeons could be sure of what was required in order to receive a food pellet, and would do so quickly) but a medium extinction rate (as the pigeons would not notice the halting of food pellet delivery as quickly as a CRF schedule but they would notice it faster than in variable schedule situations, where there is less certainty). An example of a FR schedule in humans may be a child receiving a gold star or other merit for every five words they spell correctly.

A Variable Ratio (VR) schedule involves reinforcement occurring after a random (unpredictable) number of responses each time. For example, a pigeon may receive a food pellet after pecking the disc 5 times at first, but 12 pecks may be required in the next instance, followed by 8 pecks in the following instance. VR schedules tend to produce a fast response rate and a very slow extinction rate as the unpredictability of the schedule encourages the pigeon to continuously work hard to ensure it does not miss an opportunity to receive a food pellet.

An example of a VR schedule in the human world may be certain forms of gambling such as the use of fruit machines. Here, the gambler cannot be sure if the next time they play will be when they hit the jackpot and so they may continue playing despite having made huge losses. This example serves to clearly demonstrate the addictive power of VR schedules. This was an important finding from Skinner's work and one which has not been lost on the makers of fruit machines, nor indeed any other businesses seeking to exploit this powerful means of controlling behaviour. Technology companies, for example, have used these ideas to create highly addictive systems which utilize alerts and notifications which reinforce us to constantly check our devices for messages, 'likes', and other events. Particularly since the invention of smartphones and social media, we often find ourselves reaching for our devices without even realizing we're doing it. While some might think that checking a device more frequently doesn't actually make new activity (such as receiving a message) happen any faster, it does increase the likelihood that we will see the notification as soon as it arrives. This helps to explain why, when we check our phones, we often don't just stop at checking one website or application. We might check social media, then email, and then our news feed, and so on.

Furthermore, we know that when we take the action to post a message, update our status, or upload an image or video on these different websites and applications, we increase the likelihood of receiving something rewarding in return, such as a reply, new likes or followers, or our content being shared more widely. Therefore, our actions can influence when we receive a reinforcement. This is why the schedule driving the modern-day addiction to these technologies is variable (as we never know where or when the next notification will arrive or what form it will take) but also ratio (as the more actions we take, the more likely we are to receive rewards in return). Since Skinner published his work, other psychologists have applied his ideas on the addictive nature of VR schedules to explain everything from why people engage in substance abuse to why they sometimes stay in abusive relationships. As is the case with other variable schedules though, VR schedules can be implemented in different ways and response and extinction rates will vary depending on the average number of responses required for reinforcement on each specific schedule.

Despite the fact that all of these different schedules of reinforcement demonstrated the range of ways in which *posterior* events (in the form of patterns of delivering the positive reinforcement of food) can occur and the different ways this can influence subsequent behaviour, Skinner felt that operant conditioning could operate in an even more complex manner, with an influential role for *prior* events too. In other words, the events that take place immediately *before* an operant behaviour (such as lever pressing or disk pecking) may also influence the way an organism goes on to respond to any reinforcements that follow.

Contingencies of Reinforcement

Working with rats in lever boxes, Skinner was able to demonstrate that the rats could be conditioned to only press a lever following certain 'prior events'. In other words, conditioning may only take place under certain environmental conditions, such as when a certain light was shining or specific sound was playing. In order to test this, he set his Skinner Box apparatus up so that a food pellet would only be dispensed when a light was shining. If the light was shining and the rat pressed the lever, it would receive a food pellet. However, if the light was not shining and the rat then pressed the lever, no food would be dispensed. Although initially rats would often press the lever regardless of whether the light was on or not, over time the lever-pressing when the light was not shining would be extinguished. This meant that the rat had been conditioned to press the lever only when the prior event of a light shining had indicated to the rat that lever-pressing caused food to be dispensed. Skinner called this process 'discrimination' as it demonstrates the rats had been conditioned to tell the difference between two prior stimuli: the stimuli which leads to the dispensation of food and any other stimuli which does not. The prior stimuli (a light shining), which indicates that a behavioural response will be reinforced in this way, is called an antecedent.

This process of learning to discriminate and identify antecedents that lead to reinforcement forms part of a wider concept known as 'contingencies of reinforcement'. The word contingency is used because this refers to something that depends on something else in order to happen. In the case of a rat only pressing a lever when a light is shining, the lever-pressing is contingent on the light shining because it is only when this antecedent is present that the behavioural response of lever-pressing is reinforced. This is also sometimes referred to as the 'three-term contingency' because it adds a third element to the basic operant conditioning procedure which only involved an operant behaviour (lever pressing) and a reinforcer (food). In the three-term contingency, before anything else occurs, the rat is exposed to an antecedent stimulus (the light shining) and if they then emit a specific behavioural response (press a lever), the consequence will be one of reinforcement (the delivery of food). The three-term contingency of 'Antecedent-Behaviour-Consequence' (ABC) sets the context for the organism (a rat) to learn to discriminate between different stimuli so that they only show certain behaviours when the antecedent is present.

Skinner also investigated how similar prior events could be before rats lost the ability to discriminate the antecedent from the other stimuli. One experiment involved setting the Skinner Box up so that a food pellet would only be dispensed when a specific sound (tone) was played at a specific pitch before the lever would cause food to be dispensed. This allowed Skinner to vary the pitch of the tone to test whether the rat could be conditioned to discriminate between the antecedent tone and the similar, but slightly different tones. Initially, rats would often press the lever after hearing any tone – apparently generalizing the rule of how to get food to all tones. However, over time the lever pressing following different tones that would not produce food would be extinguished, meaning the rat would only press the lever after hearing the specific tone that would enable food to be dispensed. While there was a point at which rats lost the ability to discriminate the antecedent from the other tones, the most striking finding was that rats were able to discriminate, at least to an extent, between prior events even when they were very similar in nature and had only quite subtle differences to set the antecedent apart.

Combining the concepts of contingencies and schedules of reinforcement, Skinner was even able to operate one schedule of reinforcement (an FI schedule) in the presence of one stimulus (a red key) and a different schedule of reinforcement (a VR schedule) in the presence of another stimulus (a green key). Over time, a pigeon can be conditioned to display the characteristic response rate of each schedule as soon as the stimulus (contingency of reinforcement) is presented.

Humans and Three-term Contingencies

Through demonstrating the way in which operant conditioning could operate within three-term contingency, Skinner was able to demonstrate how reinforcement had the power, not just to strengthen a behaviour generally, but to selectively strengthen behaviours in specific contexts. For example, they could now explain how a child might simultaneously learn to take turns and share possessions when playing with another child at school or in the home, while taking the ball off the opposition team when playing a ball game on a sports field. If this behaviour was rewarded on the sports field by helping them score more points but not in the classroom or at home where the teacher or parent would punish them, they would learn to be discriminative about when they behave in that particular way. Skinner had therefore shown how operant conditioning could be context-dependent, and if rats were capable of learning the differences between tones played at slightly different pitches, it stands to reason that humans may be capable of far more subtle discrimination and more complex contextual learning.

Beyond the controlled world of Skinner Boxes, however, Skinner still had the task of explaining how operant conditioning might account for the wide variability of human behaviour in the chaotic, varied, and unpredictable outside world. While he had managed to develop his theory of operant conditioning in far more elaborate ways than his behavioural predecessors had been able to, the task of explaining the complexities of human behaviour was still far beyond the reaches of his basic theory. Not only did human behaviour take place in far more complex environments than the Skinner Box, but Skinner also recognized that not all recurring behaviours in humans had been directly reinforced either.

From the day his first book, *The Behavior of Organisms*, was published, Skinner had faced widespread criticism for consistently drawing conclusions about the behaviour of 'organisms' when, in fact, his work was based almost entirely on the behaviour of laboratory rats and pigeons. Skinner responded in his paper, 'The Phylogeny and Ontogeny of Behavior' (1966), by pointing out there are many precedents for concentrating on one species in biological investigations:

> *'Mendel discovered the basic laws of genetics – in the garden pea. Morgan worked out the theory of the gene – for the fruitfly. Sherrington investigated the integrative action of the nervous system – in the dog and cat. Pavlov studied the physiological activity of the cerebral cortex – in the dog.'* (Skinner, 1966)

Nonetheless, Skinner did go on to devote a great deal of effort to accounting for the complexity of human behaviour.

Shaping Behaviour

One key concept Skinner introduced to begin to account for the variation and complexity of human behaviour is 'shaping'. This refers to the continuous and ongoing process taking place throughout our lives in which our environment makes tiny adjustments to our behaviour to mould it over time. As Skinner put it in 'Science and Human Behavior' (1953):

> *'Operant conditioning shapes behavior as a sculptor shapes a lump of clay. Although at some point the sculptor seems to have produced an entirely novel object, we can always follow the process back to the original undifferentiated lump, and we can make the successive stages by which we return to this condition as small as we wish.'* (Skinner, 1953)

Using this analogy, Skinner aimed to highlight a common error people make when trying to explain the huge variety of behaviours available to humans, as well as the wide range of behavioural differences between individuals using operant conditioning. The mistake, as Skinner saw it, was to assume operant behaviour exists in discrete units (such as lever-pressing) which emerge in their final form to be reinforced by the environment, or not, as the case may be. In reality, he argues, behaviour exists on a continuum consisting of the slightest of changes in activity whereby each tiny change could be reinforced to different degrees.

Drawing on his laboratory work with pigeons, Skinner uses the example of a pigeon being conditioned to peck a spot to further demonstrate the point. Rather than waiting for the pigeon to peck the spot which could take hours (and even then it is not guaranteed they will do it), instead he would condition the behaviour in gradual steps. In other words, the conditions (or contingencies) required to receive the reinforcement should shift each time the pigeon moves a step closer to the desired behaviour. Firstly, he would give the bird food when it turns slightly in the direction of the spot from any part of the cage. After achieving the right orientation, he would then withhold reinforcement until a slight movement is made towards the spot, continuing by reinforcing positions successively closer to the spot, then by reinforcing only when it moves its head slightly forward, and finally only when the beak makes contact with the spot. Using a process of continuously reinforcing behaviour in successive approximations like this, the desired behaviour of pecking the spot can be achieved far more quickly than would otherwise be possible.

Although the pigeon example represents Skinner's deliberate, planned conditioning of the pigeon, he proposes it is a similar continuous process through which all of our experiences as humans from childhood through to adulthood shape our behaviour. In 'Science and Human Behavior' (1953), he wrote:

> *'Through the reinforcement of slightly exceptional instances of his behavior, a child learns to raise himself, to stand, to walk, to grasp objects, and to move them about. Later on, through the same process, he learns to*

> *talk, to sing, to dance, to play games – in short, to exhibit the enormous repertoire characteristic of the normal adult.'* (Skinner, 1953)

Indeed, Skinner would go on to call volume two of his three-volume autobiography, *The Shaping of a Behaviorist* (1979).

Creating Sequences of Behaviour: Chaining

In a further effort to account for the complexities of daily human activity through operant conditioning, Skinner proposed the concept of 'chaining'. A chain occurs when one behaviour produces or alters some of the variables which control another behaviour, creating unique sequences of behaviour. For example, walking through a city centre we might look to one side and something may catch our attention, causing us to start walking in that direction. However, this involves walking up a steep hill which is tiring, leading us to abandon the movement and sit down in a coffee shop to rest, and so on. Such chains may have little or no organization but these sequences of behaviour, where each experience of reinforcement and punishment serves to shape our subsequent behaviour, may help explain much of the behaviour we think we are freely and actively driving.

In more scientific terms, chaining demonstrates that an antecedent (prior event) does not always simply function to set the occasion for a subsequent behavioural response, but it can function as a reinforcer of a preceding behaviour too. Returning to an earlier example of a contingency of reinforcement whereby the contingency of a light acted as an antecedent for lever-pressing yielding food, this three-term contingency can be extended by making the light contingent on the rat turning around when a sound is played. This results in the chain 'noise – turn-around – light – press lever – food'. Much longer chains can be built by adding more stimuli and responses, producing increasingly complex and varied behavioural sequences.

Rule-Governed Behaviour

While shaping and chaining might help to explain how a large number of behavioural variations might arise from environmental reinforcement, Skinner still recognized that a great deal of human behaviour cannot be accounted for by gradual shaping or the construction of complex sequences of behaviour. This is because, much of the time, complex behaviour in humans often appears suddenly and in its final form. For example, a person is able to navigate their way from one town to another, despite having never done it before, by following a series of directions given by a friend.

To account for such behaviour, Skinner introduced the concept of Rule-Governed Behaviour (RGB). This refers to any behaviour that has fallen under the control of verbal stimuli, with the verbal stimuli acting as the 'rule'. In the case of following directions from one town to another, the instructions the person hears act as a rule (or 'contingency-specifying' verbal formula) which governs the subsequent distances travelled and changes of direction that the person makes at certain points in order to reach their destination. After successfully implementing the rule (by arriving at the destination), this successful outcome may then serve to reinforce the behaviour.

Tracing the development of such RGB back to early childhood, it is clear to see how behaviour might begin to fall under verbal control. To begin with, it is only relatively simple behaviours which come under the control of verbal stimuli. For example, a child may learn to follow instructions such as 'push', 'pull', 'don't touch', 'don't run', 'turn the page' or 'press the button', and so on. As a child's experiences and vocabulary increase, more and more behavioural responses will fall under such verbal control, meaning longer sequences of verbal stimuli will eventually acquire the power to evoke an almost unlimited variety of complex behavioural responses.

Skinner went on to explain the complexities of language acquisition and development in his book, *Verbal Behavior*. This specific application of his ideas and many others form the basis of the following chapter which covers everything from pigeon-guided missiles to teaching machines.

4. Applications of Skinner's Work

While Skinner's theoretical work was extensive, with the previous chapter only offering a brief insight into his account of behaviour, Skinner was far from satisfied by merely describing and explaining behaviour; he wanted to modify it, shape it and control it. In his laboratory work, Skinner had always demonstrated a hands-on approach to experimentation. The Skinner Box, along with different schedules and contingencies of reinforcement, had given him the means to precisely control the behaviour of rats and pigeons, but he soon wanted this control and influence to reach beyond the laboratory to help create a better world. Throughout his career, Skinner had been an active proponent of the view that his science of behaviour should be used across human society and he dedicated huge amounts of time and effort to various applications of his work, albeit some with more success than others. Nonetheless, all of this work serves to demonstrate his unwavering belief in the power of behavioural science to solve all manner of real-world problems.

Behaviour Modification

One of Skinner's biggest contributions to solving real-world problems came in his founding of a school of experimental research psychology – the experimental analysis of behaviour – and development of behaviour modification (which later became known as Applied Behaviour Analysis, or ABA). Behaviour modification refers to a set of techniques based on operant conditioning that seek to change environmental conditions that are related to a person's behaviour. Some specific examples of areas in which behaviour modification and ABA have been used include forms of therapy practised in psychiatric hospitals, prisons, and education (particularly in schools for children with special educational needs such as autism).

In settings such as these, operant conditioning techniques have been applied through the use of primary and secondary reinforcers. Primary reinforcers refer to anything which can be used to strengthen behaviour by itself without the need for learning (for example, food or comfort), whereas secondary reinforcers refer to anything which can be exchanged for primary reinforcers (points or tokens) and therefore have to acquire their value through association with primary reinforcers. These ideas can be used to establish a 'token economy' whereby tokens in the form of coloured counters, for example, can be used as secondary reinforcers to reinforce a set of desired behaviours in a group of target individuals. These tokens can then be exchanged by those individuals in exchange for primary reinforcers (treats or time for enjoyable activities).

In a psychiatric hospital, for example, token economy systems such as this have been used to encourage patients to begin the process of recovery from severe mental illness by showing desired behaviours such as getting out of bed, brushing their teeth, making their bed and, eventually, helping with other chores around their ward. In prison, inmates might be rewarded with tokens for behaving appropriately and helpfully in different situations, and in schools, children's positive behaviour can be reinforced in a similar manner by the teachers. In these settings, target behaviours are not expected to emerge in their final form immediately and, instead, behaviour can be acquired in steps. For example, if the target behaviour for someone is to maintain their attention for a 30 minute session, they might initially receive reinforcement (a token) for maintaining their attention for 5 minutes. Once this has been reliably achieved, they might then only be reinforced for paying attention for 10 minutes, and so on until they reach the target. This process is an application of Skinner's concept of shaping.

While behaviour modification and ABA have been applied successfully in a wide range of contexts, they are also all examples of closely controlled settings. The advantage of such settings is that those in charge, whether they are hospital managers, prison superintendents, or teachers, have the ability to closely monitor behaviour and consistently administer schedules of reinforcement. One common criticism of token economies such as these is that they simply would not work outside of such controlled situations where behaviour cannot be consistently monitored and reinforced in the same way. Nonetheless, Skinner's ideas have inspired a huge amount of research and the development of new techniques that have gone on to benefit numerous professionals and their clients in a range of settings.

While it is difficult to think of many theories in psychology that have been applied to such a broad spectrum of specialist areas such as Skinner's have, it is even more difficult to think of a psychologist who has personally worked on such a unique and varied series of applied research projects as Skinner. Few scientists can claim to have applied their theories to everything from the care of new-born babies to the development of military weapons systems, but then few share the bold willingness of Skinner to turn their ideas into solutions to real-world problems, no matter the conundrum.

Project Pigeon

Skinner's first personal opportunity to move his theory of operant conditioning outside the Skinner Box and into the real-world was inspired, of all things, by the horrors of World War II. Reading about the devastation caused by the bombs and missiles of aeroplanes and warships, Skinner had wondered whether a solution could be developed to stop these explosives at source. He later remarked that the idea of using birds as part of such a solution first came to him in April 1940, while looking out of a train window on his way to a Midwestern Psychological Association meeting. In *The Shaping of a Behaviorist*, he later reflected:

> *'I saw a flock of birds lifting and wheeling in formation as they flew alongside the train. Suddenly I saw them as "devices" with excellent vision and extraordinary manoeuvrability. Could they not guide a missile?'* (Skinner, 1979)

On his return home, he found a poultry shop that sold pigeons to Chinese restaurants and bought a few. This was how pigeons became Skinner's bird of choice. He discovered that he could easily restrain their wings and feet by slipping them into a toeless sock and was impressed with the range of behaviours the pigeons could perform with remarkable accuracy while restrained in this manner, if reinforced after pecking. As a result, pigeons would soon supersede rats as Skinner's research subject of choice. By 'shaping' the pigeon's pecking behaviour on a step-by-step basis, Skinner found he could quickly condition them to perform a variety of relatively complex behaviours. For example, he taught them to play a simple tune on a four-key piano and even conditioned two pigeons to play ping-pong. In fact, teaching pigeons to play ping-pong could be accomplished in just three steps: reinforcing them when they were near the ball, then only when they pecked the ball, and then only when they pecked the ball to the other side of the purpose-built pigeon ping-pong table (where their conditioned opponent could return their shots).

Although Skinner's concept of pigeon-guided missiles was initially rejected by the National Defense Research Committee (NDRC), he did manage to get funding of $5,000 from the General Mills Company to develop his device up to a point where government funding might be possible. After being granted a sabbatical in January 1942 from the University of Minnesota where he was working at the time, Skinner began work on his concept and, by September, had in effect become a full-time employee of the General Mills Company. He moved all research activity to the top floor of a flour mill in Minneapolis where he, along with his team of talented students, began intensively training pigeons to peck targets in a manner that could later be incorporated into a missile device.

NDRC officials visited General Mills in the spring of 1943 and, despite some concerns over the eccentricity and

Fig. 8 A pigeon is guided into a glide missile, as part of Skinner's Project Pigeon, 1943.

impracticality of the idea, were sufficiently encouraged to award Skinner and his team a $25,000 contract to do the top-secret work of developing the pigeon-guided missile. With Project Pigeon now in full swing, work began to control the handling of the pigeons by a hydraulic pickup and, later, by a pneumatic device. A metal conductor would be attached to the bird's beak so that its pecks could be transmitted to the missile guidance system. The plan was for the pigeon to be situated inside a glide missile, restrained in a manner which closely resembled Skinner's original toeless sock. The pigeon would be suspended within pecking distance of a window through which they would be able to see the desired target, such as a warship in the sea. Just as it had been reinforced in the laboratory for pecking moving targets on a screen, the pigeon's pecking of the target in the window would send messages to control the tail fins of the missile to ensure it stayed on course and, ultimately, hit its target.

The success in getting Project Pigeon to this stage may have been seen by Skinner as vindication of his idea. Indeed, NDRC observers did recommend an additional $30,000 to help Skinner perfect the weapon, but this was rejected by headquarters in Washington D.C., without an explanation being provided. In meetings between Skinner and the NDRC that followed, questions over the stability of the pigeon-guided missile were cited as concerns. However, a huge part of their decision must have been influenced by the technological alternatives the United States had in development. Cruise missiles which incorporated gyroscope guidance had been around since World War I. At a time when unprecedented levels of investment were going into technology such as the atomic bomb, investing in animal-guided devices at all seems like a bizarre and old-fashioned route to have taken. Furthermore, as all of Skinner's Project Pigeon work was classified, when the mainstream American public were first introduced to Skinner's well-trained pigeons in the 1950s, there was no reference to their proposed war-time duties. Instead, the media preferred to focus on the fact that his pigeons could play ping-pong and piano. Skinner's huge disappointment at the NDRC's decision and the end of his wartime project, however, could not detract from his achievements in getting to the point he did, and his overall optimism for the practical potential of his ideas.

Innovating Childcare Solutions: The Aircrib

Skinner's desire to address more real-world problems soon had a new focus, albeit a problem that was far less extreme. The inspiration behind this focus had originally come from his wife,

Yvonne. In 1944, when she was expecting their second child, Deborah, Yvonne had spoken to Skinner about her concerns that typical baby tenders (or cribs) posed a number of risks to babies. For example, she felt that the bars could trap a baby's leg and the blankets had the potential to suffocate a baby. In addition to these concerns, there was another motivation for Skinner here too. In his professional career, he had spent years designing and re-designing his Skinner Boxes in response to the behaviour of rats and then pigeons. His designs, however, had not merely been made to help produce better experimental results, but also to facilitate better, more simplified care of the animals inside. As well as testing the animals, Skinner had to regularly clean their boxes and prepare their food and so making this as straightforward as possible was to the benefit of both the researchers and animals alike. After having taken on a number of the traditionally maternal chores following the birth of their first daughter, Julie, Skinner was keen to do all he could to make life as simple, comfortable, and risk-free as possible with their second, and so he quietly set to work on his baby tender.

Fig. 9 Skinner's daughter Deborah in the baby tender, or 'aircrib', 1944.

After an initial period of trial and error, Skinner finally settled on a design. His baby tender was a thermostatically controlled, air-filtered, enclosed space with sound-absorbing walls (which would still allow the baby to be heard from every room in the house), a stretched canvas floor and a safety glass window (with a curtain to shut out light). While conventional cribs consisted of a thick mattress and a need for the baby to be wrapped up which restricted their movement, the aim with this design was to provide a freedom of movement that wasn't possible before, while maintaining the child's protection and safety. Furthermore, the stretched canvas floor was actually only one section of a strip of sheeting ten yards long. Not only did this serve as a mattress for the baby but it was easy to keep clean too as a new clean section could be cranked into place in a few seconds. Skinner had created a new, controlled environment for early childcare that could help parents by simplifying the task of caring for their baby and, in doing so, freeing up time for them to focus on enhancing their bond.

Deborah Skinner would spend a lot of time in her father's new crib in the early part of her life. Proud of his invention and confident of its commercial potential too, Skinner entered a phase of discussion and negotiation with a range of possible manufacturers who might be able to take his product to market. As part of his attempts to raise the profile of his baby tender (or aircrib as it had become known by this point), he sent an article to the popular magazine, *Lady's Home Journal*. In order to create more interest though, the magazine article referred to the aircrib as 'Baby in a Box', inevitably leading to assumptions that Skinner was treating his baby daughter in the same way he treated his laboratory rats in the Skinner Box. Despite being completely untrue, these rumours plagued Skinner for the rest of his life, going so far as to even suggest (quite falsely) that Deborah had gone on to take her own life. The association between the aircrib and the Skinner Box was probably also a key reason for Skinner's ultimate failure to make the product a success. Nonetheless, Julie (his first daughter) went on to raise Skinner's granddaughter in an aircrib, just as he had done with Deborah.

Teaching Machines

The aircrib wasn't the only invention of Skinner's that was inspired by Deborah. On 11 November 1953, when she was in Fourth Grade at school, Skinner was invited to attend her mathematics class for Father's Day. While sitting at the back of her typical mainstream school classroom, Skinner had an epiphany. As he would later explain, 'through no fault of her own the teacher was violating almost everything we knew about the learning process' (Vargas, *B.F. Skinner Foundation*). Through his work in the laboratory, Skinner was quite aware that, in order for learners to make progress, the teacher must adapt what they are asking of the learner to their current performance level (or, as Skinner put it, the 'animal's current performance level', viewing learning in children in much the same way as learning in any other animal). Despite this, Skinner could see that while some of the students had no idea how to solve the problems which were clearly beyond their current performance level, others whipped through the exercise sheet as it was way below their ability level. What this meant was that the students on either end of the spectrum of ability were learning nothing new. Skinner knew from his work that learners progress most effectively when each best response is immediately reinforced. In the school classroom environment, however, it was simply not possible for one teacher to provide such immediate reinforcement, tailored to each individual's

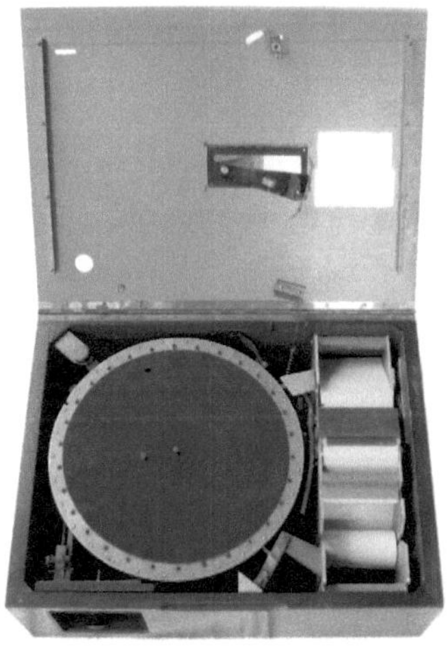

Fig. 10 An example of one of Skinner's teaching machines.

current performance level in a class of 20 or 30 schoolchildren. It was clear to Skinner that something different was needed and this was the inspiration for his first teaching machine.

In order to truly personalize learning for each individual learner, Skinner planned to create a machine that every child could have at their desk, and which could meet each of their individual learning needs. Skinner wasted no time and, just a few days after his school visit, he had already created an initial prototype. His single-minded, hands-on approach to problem-solving was evident yet again. The prototype was known as a 'slider machine' and it was invented primarily to teach spelling and arithmetic. He had printed a series of maths problems on cards which could be placed in the machine. Each question had a two-digit solution which the student would attempt to answer by moving two levers. If they were right, a light would appear in a hole in the card, giving immediate reinforcement, and the chance to move through problems at their own individual pace. To prevent students from cheating by moving the sliders to find the correct answers, the levers would lock into place once selected. While clearly limited in the types of problems (and therefore the types of learning) for which this machine could be used, it did give Skinner a starting point from which to build. This was soon followed by machines that could generate problems printed on pleated tape and later on cardboard disks. These problems always started in relatively straightforward fashion before becoming increasingly difficult to continuously engage and challenge students using them.

Skinner was not the first to create a teaching machine. Sidney Pressey (1888–1979) had been the first psychologist to build one back in 1926, with his invention taking the form of a box with a revolving drum which rotated to reveal a question, and buttons with which to respond. Pressey's device wasn't programmed according to the principles of operant conditioning, nor did it catch on at the time, leaving Skinner as the foremost developer of the teaching machine in the 1950s. However, the machines were only a device and therefore could only be as good as the content it displayed. In order to promote effective learning, Skinner recognized that there was a need for programmed instruction for these devices to deliver. In effect, he was proposing that teaching needed to become scientifically designed, structured, and pre-scripted, in order for it to be automated. In this way each individual in the school classroom would be able to reach their full potential.

Priming and Vanishing

In order to develop his notion of programmed instruction, Skinner began breaking down the role of the teacher into basic techniques; each could then be automated in some way. For example, he identified 'priming' as one such technique. This involved the teacher first showing students what to do in order for them to then follow (in this way the children were 'primed' before trying themselves). Another technique was 'vanishing', which

Skinner first tried out on Deborah when she had to memorize lines from a piece of literature for homework. He wrote out the passage in question and let her read it before sending her out of the room. He immediately began erasing a number of letters from the words in the passage so that, when she returned, she would have to remember the passage even with letters missing. Skinner later remarked that, after five or six erasures, there was no writing left and yet Deborah was still able to 'read' the passage. He incorporated vanishing into the design of his next teaching machine whereby a sheet of text could be inserted, followed by sheets of clear plastic with obscuring lines or spots to gradually make more and more parts of the text vanish.

Skinner would spend the next ten years heavily involved in the teaching machine movement. There was huge interest among educationalists in Skinner's ideas, particularly his concept of programmed instruction. The practical reality of producing teaching machines that could offer programmed instruction, however, presented a number of difficulties which led to most being put into book form instead, even though this lacked many of the benefits of using a machine. For this reason, by 1968 – the year that Skinner published his book, *The Technology of Teaching* – publishers stopped printing programmed instruction altogether. Although some of Skinner's programmes are still used today, his ideas have ultimately been realized with the creation of computers and the Internet. In the same way Project Pigeon had been eclipsed by advancing military technologies in warfare, so too were teaching machines ultimately superseded by computers. Nonetheless, many of the online courses of today put into practice ideas which were developed by Skinner before the online world existed.

Beyond teaching machines and programmed instruction, Skinner has had a huge influence on education. He believed that the goal for teachers and other educationalists should be to find ways to make education effective for all students, and that the best way to modify and shape learner behaviour was to modify the environment. Skinner was a proponent for many instructional strategies that form part of teacher training and professional development to this day. These strategies include the scaffolding (or gradual building) of instructions, completion of work in small units, regular repetition and review of instructions, and immediate feedback. Skinner did not approve of the use of punishments in school, or as a behaviour modification technique in general, instead promoting the frequent and consistent use of reinforcement to shape learner behaviour. Many of the classroom strategies he advocated formed part of the schedules of reinforcement and shaping techniques that had proven so powerful in other settings.

Verbal Behaviour

Throughout the time of his involvement in the various practical projects covered in this chapter, he had been working on possibly the most challenging application of all his concepts. While his theories based on the behaviour of rats and pigeons in the laboratory could be plausibly extended to those of humans in a number of real-world situations, language was always considered to be too complex and fundamentally too human for such theories to expound. This may go some way to explain why it took him around 20 years to write the book *Verbal Behavior* (notwithstanding the fact he had in this time been working on a range of other projects!).

Despite having a love for language and literature throughout his life, his interest in explaining language from a behaviourist perspective can be traced back to his time as a Junior Fellow at Harvard when the philosopher Alfred North Whitehead had challenged him to explain a randomly provided piece of verbal behaviour. He began collecting samples of verbal performance in 1934 and, together with his wife Yvonne, Skinner would go on to record and analyze a great deal of their daughters' early language use too. While the book included these attempts to gather evidence, *Verbal Behavior* would go on to differ a great deal from Skinner's other books in that it is largely theoretical, at times difficult to read, and involves little experimental research. Indeed, it would take a number of years before a growing body of research into the ideas presented in the book would emerge.

Skinner's account of how the complexities of language develop maintains the same basic approach he had previously taken to explaining how any other behaviour arises. Namely, that it develops as a result of its functional relationships to the environment in which it occurs. In the same way that a rat might press a lever as a result of a controlling antecedent (a light shining) and/or a controlling consequence (food reinforcement) in the Skinner Box environment, similarly, a word, phrase or sentence might be spoken as a result of a controlling antecedent and/or consequence in a real-life human situation.

In *Verbal Behavior* Skinner introduces what he calls 'the six verbal operant behaviours': mand, tact, audience relation, echoic, textual, and intraverbal; each of which he outlines in detail. A mand, for example, is a verbal operant that occurs as a result of a motivating operation (experiencing satiation or deprivation) which acts as the controlling antecedent and/or the consequence of the mand. A mand is typically a demand, command, or request and therefore they often explicitly specify the consequence. For example, a child saying to their mother 'I want milk' is a mand because the verbal behaviour occurs due to the antecedent of thirst (or the motivating operation of deprivation) which would usually then be reinforced when the mother provides the child with the milk.

Not all verbal operants arise as the result of a motivating operation in this way, however; most do not, and nor do they always need to be directly reinforced, as in the example of a mand. Some of the other operants occur in response to the antecedent of a verbal stimulus from another person, such as during a conversation, and the consequence may come in a more social form, such as agreement, praise, or laughter, for example. Skinner did not claim that all verbal behaviour must be one or other of his verbal operants. In fact, he was keen to point out that very little verbal behaviour consists of these *pure* operants, and that most consist of a mixture of them.

Criticism of *Verbal Behavior*

Skinner's account of verbal behaviour in his book of the same name has influenced a range of researchers and academics since its publication in 1957. It has also come in for some notable criticism. In 1959, Noam Chomsky wrote an influential critique of Skinner's work. Among other criticisms, he questioned how Skinner could account for the fact that children acquire early language without being overtly *taught* and that people can both speak and understand sentences that they have never heard before. Chomsky's review has since come to be regarded as one of the foundational documents of the discipline of Cognitive Psychology; an approach to psychological research that rose to prominence around this time leading many to question Skinner's behaviourist approach.

As mainstream psychology became increasingly dominated by the cognitive approach in the 1960s and 70s, the focus of attempts to study and explain human behaviour returned once more to internal states and mental processes. This was the very focus that the early behaviourists, Pavlov and Watson, had been so keen to move away from. Nonetheless, Skinner's work and his influence was far from diminished and he continued to produce research that brought many of the assumptions of the cognitive approach into doubt.

Teaching Pigeons to Talk

The shift towards humanistic and cognitive psychology had, for many, consigned the behaviourist preference for animal research to the history books. The humanistic view of every human being as a unique, active agent in their own behaviour directly contradicted the assumptions made by Skinner and clearly positioned humans as a special case among other animals. Likewise, the cognitive focus on mental processes like thinking, memory, and language led to a rise in psychological testing whereby the topics studied, and methods used to study them, were almost entirely human-centred. However, Skinner was keen to demonstrate the flaws in these approaches. He felt that the tendency to view human behaviour, including our language, as being unique to humans or the result of conscious, free will, was just an illusion and that, just because we may feel like we are in active control of our thinking and behaviour does not mean that this is true. To illustrate this point, he conducted a series of tests in which even some of the most apparently human of abilities, such as talking and a sense of self-concept, could be demonstrated by pigeons under the right environmental conditions.

One experiment Skinner conducted in 1980, together with psychologist Robert Epstein (1953–) and scientist Robert Lanza (1956–), was named 'Symbolic Communication between Two Pigeons' but is sometimes referred to as the 'Jack and Jill Experiment'. Skinner and Epstein placed two pigeons (named Jack and Jill) in a box, separated from each other by a window. Jack would peck a sign on the wall which said 'What colour?', making it light up. On seeing this through the window, Jill would thrust her head through a curtain on the wall where a colour would now be illuminated that was either green, yellow, or red. As this colour was displayed behind a curtain, Jack would not be able to see which colour Jill had seen from her side of the box. Jill would then have to indicate to Jack which colour she had seen behind the curtain by pecking one of three neutral-coloured letter keys: 'G' for Green, 'Y' for Yellow, or 'R' for Red. On seeing which one of these letters lit up after being pecked, Jack would peck a sign on the wall which said 'thank you', which would dispense a food pellet for Jill. Jack would then peck the coloured button on his side corresponding to the letter which Jill had communicated to him. This would dispense a food pellet for him to eat. This demonstration showed how, following a period of initial behaviour shaping, pigeons were capable of being conditioned to produce a chained series of exchanges from one bird to the next in a manner which very much resembled a basic form of conversation. They had been conditioned to talk!

Skinner and Epstein were also able to condition pigeons in a similar fashion to demonstrate a sense of self-concept and creative thinking. While these demonstrations may be relatively short, and carefully planned and executed, nonetheless they do offer a brief glimpse of the possibilities. Many of the cognitive abilities, thought of as too human and too complex for the animal-derived theory of operant conditioning to explain, might not be beyond the scope of Skinnerian behaviourism after all.

5. Radical Behaviourism

While Skinner shared much in common with his behaviourist predecessors, such as Pavlov and Watson, none of them had the same impact on society as Skinner. But it wasn't his laboratory research, his theory of operant conditioning, or his Skinner Boxes that made national headline news. Nor was it his commercial ventures with the aircrib, his teaching machines, or his pigeon-guided missiles that led to his public notoriety. Instead, it was his broader philosophy known as radical behaviourism – the philosophy of the science of behaviour – that would go on to have the biggest influence.

Yet, in many respects, radical behaviourism has a great deal in common with the previous forms of behaviourism. By the time Skinner's controversial book, *Beyond Freedom and Dignity* (1971), had landed him in the media spotlight, the theories of Pavlov and Watson had been around for over half a century. All of these behaviourists were in agreement that the environment plays a far greater role in moulding human behaviour than had previously been suggested. They also agreed that experiments should focus on observable, external actions if psychological science is to be a truly objective field that can be trusted.

Indeed, Watson's behaviourist manifesto of 1913 – 'Psychology as the Behaviorist Views It' – had sought to shift the focus of psychological research away from what he saw as the subjective study of internal, private events such as thoughts and feelings towards a more objective science. After all, this was why they were known as behaviourists. Although Watson's 'methodological behaviourism' (as Skinner referred to it) still acknowledged that thoughts and feelings exist, he felt that their private nature placed them outside the scope of a science of behaviour. In *Behaviorism* (1925), Watson wrote that 'the Behaviourist must exclude from his scientific vocabulary all subjective terms such as sensation, perception, image, desire, purpose, and even thinking and emotion as they were subjectively defined'.

Skinner's radical behaviourism, however, redefined behaviour to include 'everything that an organism does', including thinking, feeling and speaking, and argued that these phenomena were all valid subject matters for behavioural science. In fact, the term 'radical behaviourism' refers to just this: that *everything* an organism does is a behaviour. Skinner agreed with Watson that experimental analysis should confine itself to observable and manipulable events, but he differed from Watson in proposing that the scope of the principles derived from this experimental analysis include all behavioural events – those that are internal and those that are external.

Over the years, many textbooks have inaccurately portrayed these distinctions between Watson's methodological behaviourism and Skinner's radical behaviourism. Perhaps in trying to emphasize that Skinner held behaviour to be the proper subject matter of psychology, these books have often failed to clarify Skinner's position and have suggested, implicitly or otherwise, that Skinner ruled out the study of private events as unscientific. This was Watson's position, but not Skinner's. In many ways then, radical behaviourism goes further than methodological behaviourism by suggesting that environmental variables control even these private, internal events just as they control observable behaviours. In other words, just as the environment has the power to shape our behaviour, it can shape our innermost thoughts and feelings too.

Although Skinner incorporated thinking and feeling into his radical behaviourist philosophy, he ruled them out as valid explanations of behaviour. His reasoning for this was that these internal events were viewed much in the same way as external actions: they were behaviours. For Skinner, the practice of explaining behaviour by referring to thought or feelings, as employed by those in the field of mentalism, represented a pseudo-explanation because they merely point to more behaviour needing to be explained. Skinner maintained that whether behaviours are internal or external, environmental factors are the proper causes of behaviour.

Misconceptions of Radical Behaviourism

While the publication of *Beyond Freedom and Dignity* in 1971 marked a watershed moment for Skinner in terms of the reaction his ideas provoked (in the American public at least), his philosophy of radical behaviourism had faced criticism throughout his career. During all this time, he maintained that a reason for much of this hostility was a lack of understanding of his position, and a series of common misconceptions.

One misconception is that Skinner's radical behaviourism took a positivist approach to scientific research. This is the idea that the world can be objectively known. However, for all of Skinner's emphasis on the need for experiments to focus only on the visible and measurable behaviour of organisms, he never claimed this would offer objective knowledge of the world. He acknowledged that the scientific research of a radical behaviourist was a human activity and, as such, it was subject to the same contextual analysis as any other behaviour. In other words, the researcher was subject to contingencies of reinforcement and had been shaped by them in much the same way he was setting up his own contingencies to test the behaviour of other organisms. Radical behaviourism views science, not as a means of discovering the 'truth' which no science can deliver, but as a method for better understanding and relating to the world.

Another misconception of Skinner's philosophy, as he saw it, was its inability to explain our most human characteristics that set us aside from rats and pigeons. Critics have portrayed Skinner's theories as a set of responses to stimuli that treat humans as mere machines, ignoring our states of mind, consciousness, cognitive processes, sense of self, personality, morality, intentions and purpose. However, Skinner felt many of these criticisms stemmed from the lasting impression left by Watson's earlier form of behaviourism. It was Watson's attempts to shift the focus in psychology away from internal processes that lead to Skinner's consideration of these processes being overlooked. It also invited the critique that Watson's shift was only necessary because behaviourism lacked the depth to explain such complex functions. This may explain why Skinner's explicit attempts to explain issues like morality and language development, from a radical behaviourist perspective, may have, to an extent, fallen on deaf ears.

Related to this, another misconception of radical behaviourism is that it suggests organisms (including humans) are passive receivers of conditioning. In this sense, many critics have portrayed Skinner's view of human behaviour as being purely reactive even though many human behaviours appear quite suddenly, spontaneously, and unpredictably. For this reason, critics have suggested Skinner's theories cannot explain creative behaviour such as art, music, or literature. However, this portrayal misrepresents Skinner by failing to take into account that operant behaviour is called 'operant' because it operates *on* the environment. In other words, a range of behaviours are emitted, not elicited, and animals can act on the environment as much as the environment acts back. This is why active and spontaneous creations of art, music, or poetry can be emitted and, if they are reinforced by the positive reactions of observers, listeners, or readers, the likelihood of further creativity will be increased.

One final misconception that applies, not only to radical behaviourism, but to forms of behaviourism in general, is that they suggest the new-born infant is a tabula rasa (blank slate). By focusing on the role the environment plays in moulding behaviour, many believed behaviourists were espousing a view that all behaviour comes from our interactions with the environment, therefore ignoring the role of genetic inheritance and evolution in behaviour. In fact, neither Watson, Pavlov, nor Skinner ignored the role of genes and physiology in behaviour. It is highly possible that this misconception arose from Watson's famous 'dozen healthy infants' quote (see Chapter 2) and which routinely appears in texts offering an introduction to behaviourism. In quoting only part of Watson's statement, writers presented his methodological form of behaviourism as having an extreme and blinkered view of the importance of environment, and this view has also led to Skinner's radical behaviourism, by extension, being misrepresented despite its important differences. Far from ignoring or rejecting the role of genes and evolution in behaviour, Skinner's radical behaviourism does acknowledge their role and this forms a key part of understanding radical behaviourism.

Shaping Behaviour Over Generations

'The Phylogeny and Ontogeny of Behavior' was originally published in the journal *Science* in 1966. Its comprehensive discussion of the role played by evolution, as well as environmental reinforcement, in the development of behaviour should have banished any misconceptions around Skinner's views in this area. 'Ontogeny' refers to the development of an organism's characteristics and behaviour throughout its lifespan, whereas 'phylogeny' refers to the development of characteristics and behaviour through the evolutionary history of the species. Therefore, characteristics and behaviours which have been shaped over generations via natural selection may be said to have been shaped by phylogenic contingencies. This may be the case for the intricate web-spinning behaviours of spiders that seem too complex to have been shaped through operant conditioning during the relatively short duration of the lifetime of an individual spider. However, when an individual organism does change its behaviour to adapt to changes in its environment during its lifetime, this speed of change and adaptation must have been shaped by ontogenic contingencies through a process of operant conditioning. Such changes in behaviour were clearly demonstrated by Skinner in the carefully shaped behaviours of rats and pigeons in the unfamiliar environment of his Skinner Box. The reason Skinner favoured the study of ontogenic change over phylogenic change was precisely because it could be studied directly in the evolutionary present, without the need for any assumptions about how phylogenic contingencies may have functioned in the distant past.

Skinner and Darwin

Skinner's radical behaviourism does explain human behaviour within a Darwinian framework. Just as Darwin had explained how species adapt to their environments over generations through a process of natural selection, Skinner explained how individual organisms adapt to their environments within their lifetimes through a process of operant conditioning. In fact, Skinner has even been described as the 'Darwin of ontogeny' (Donahoe, 1984). However, because both ontogeny and phylogeny ultimately serve a similar purpose – to enable the organism to adapt to its environment – they are not always easy to disentangle. Skinner explained this difficulty in his paper, 'The Phylogeny and Ontogeny of Behavior', by saying:

> *'With respect to phylogenic contingencies, this is what is meant by natural selection. With respect to ontogeny, it is what is meant by operant conditioning. Successful responses are selected in both cases, and the result is adaptation. But the processes of selection are very*

> *different, and we cannot tell from the mere fact that behavior is adaptive which kind of process has been responsible for it.'* (Skinner, 1966)

Skinner did spend time discussing the ways in which these two types of contingency might operate, including the possible ways in which behaviours of phylogenic origin can interfere with operant conditioning and vice versa. To do this, Skinner drew on the work of Breland and Breland, a husband and wife team of behavioural psychologists who had both trained under Skinner and worked with him on Project Pigeon, before specializing in using operant conditioning to develop humane animal training methods. The Brelands conditioned a chicken to deliver plastic capsules containing small toys to a customer by moving them with one or two sharp, straight pecks. However, despite some success they reported that often the chicken would begin to grab at the capsules and 'pound them up and down on the floor of the cage' (Breland & Breland, 1961), perhaps as if they were breaking seed pods or pieces of food too large to be swallowed as chickens may have done in their evolutionary past. This may well show that operant conditioning can be effective but that genetically inherited, evolutionary traits shaped by phylogenic contingencies can impact on ontogenic contingencies of reinforcement. This was a conclusion Skinner referred to as 'plausible, and not disturbing' (Skinner, 1966).

To demonstrate a possible reversal of this relationship, Skinner cites an example from Project Pigeon, in which a hungry pigeon that was being trained to guide missiles was reinforced with food on a schedule of reinforcement which generated a very high rate of pecking at a target. However, when it then tried to eat, the pigeon began to peck at the food as rapidly as it had been conditioned to peck the target, which was too fast to permit it to take grains into its mouth, and it began to starve. This would seem to show how a product of ontogenic contingencies had suppressed one of the most powerful phylogenic activities in eating behaviour.

Extending these ideas to human examples, a parent caring for and protecting their child could be an example of phylogenic contingencies overpowering those which are ontogenic. While dedicating huge amounts of time, energy, and sleepless nights to the care of a new-born child may not offer obvious reinforcement to the parent, especially when the child is too young to reciprocate that care or affection, it does quite clearly have huge survival value for the species as a whole. Therefore the phylogenic explanation in instances such as this does appear to have greater explanatory power. It should be stated here that attachment formation between a parent and child can and has been explained from a purely learned perspective, albeit without the level of research support enjoyed by phylogenic explanations.

Examples of ontogenic contingencies overpowering phylogenic ones in human behaviour are also easy to identify. For example, Skinner argued that ontogenic contingencies are more likely to generate behaviours which damage the behaver. This is because submitting to damaging consequences can, at times, lead to ultimate positive reinforcement. For example, hurting oneself may lead to others feeling sorry for us and giving us attention. Alternatively, submitting to damaging consequences may enable us to escape consequences which are even more damaging. For example, Skinner proposed that contingencies arranged by a culture or religion 'which makes much of personal honour' might make breaking that code of honour such a damaging, punishing prospect that even the most maladaptive of behaviours may become likely, such as 'mortification and maceration as well as martyrdom' (Skinner, 1966). In this way the ontogenic contingencies of operant conditioning may enable to us to explain why people go on hunger strike, set themselves on fire, or carry out a suicide bombing.

Furthermore, in the same way that ontogenic contingencies have the power to harm the survival of the individual, Skinner was keen to highlight that they also have the power to threaten our entire species. Climate change which poses such a threat may be seen to stem from a number of reinforced human behaviours. Examples may include the reinforcement we receive for living in centrally-heated or air-conditioned environments powered by polluting power stations. Or driving polluting cars rather than taking the time and effort to walk or cycle. Another threat to the species could be the possibility of extreme warfare. The continual reinforcement of escalating military power through its ability to offer defence and protection has led to the development of nuclear weapons which may ultimately lead to the destruction of life on earth. Skinner argues that if such apocalyptic predictions turn out to be true, 'practices which up to now have had survival value, although of ontogenic origin, would then prove to have been lethal' (Skinner, 1966). Skinner felt strongly that this accidental slide into disaster could only be avoided if we acknowledge the contingencies of reinforcement which are shaping them, and reorganize those contingencies to reverse these trends. For the radical behaviourist, changing our behaviour begins with changing our environment.

Cultural Design

Skinner was unashamedly utopian in his ambition for radical behaviourism. In the same way many criticize science for its role in developing military weapons or other damaging technologies, Skinner was keen to stress it had the same power to make a safer, fairer, and more sustainable world. Having proved the power that contingencies of reinforcement have in shaping behaviour, Skinner could not understand why we would allow the environments of our towns, cities, and broader cultures to be left to the beliefs, manners and customs of the past. Or, as he says in 'Science and Human Behavior', to the 'personal idiosyncrasies' of one strong political or religious leader after another over time. In this book, he asks:

> *'Why should the design of a culture be left so largely to accident? Is it not possible to change the social environment deliberately so that the human product will meet more acceptable specifications?'* (Skinner, 1953)

As the scientific understanding of human behaviour gathers momentum, along with our understanding of the contingencies which produce happiness, security and knowledge, for example, Skinner argued that we will have the power to design a culture that can produce these effects in everyone. The suggestion that science could or should be used to 'control' the behaviour of a society in this way is controversial to many, and Skinner wrote at length about people's criticisms and concerns about designing such a culture. He acknowledged that, in the past, leaders have attempted to use behavioural control of a coercive nature to control populations, such as in Nazi Germany. He understood that a science of behaviour does not contain within itself any means of controlling how it will be used. However, Skinner was keen to use such concerns to warn people of the dangers of *not* using a science of behaviour to design a culture that serves the masses, because a failure to do so would mean others with 'restricted interests' (such as the Nazis) surely would.

While Skinner had the grandest of utopian ambitions for radical behaviourism, he also acknowledged that designing a culture would be most effective, at least to begin with, on a smaller scale. A small-scale version of utopia was precisely what he described in his 1948 novel, *Walden Two*.

Walden Two

In his book, Skinner created an intentional community of about 1,000 members, named Walden Two, designed by a self-proclaimed genius called Frazier, who had deserted academic psychology for behavioural engineering. Frazier invites a group of people to stay with him for several days, including a soldier who has recently returned from the war, a psychology professor called Burris, and a philosophy and ethics professor, called Castle. Frazier presents the happy and hard-working community members to his visitors, explaining how they have had their behaviour carefully shaped using behavioural techniques.

Walden Two offers a glimpse of the kind of cultural design advocated by Skinner. The community's design is flexible as it is based on a model of continually testing the most successful, evidence-based strategies to employ. It also follows a carefully planned programme of 'behavioural engineering' begun at birth. Despite behaviour being engineered in this way during childhood, Frazier verifies the success of the design by pointing to the fact that the members of Walden Two are legitimately peaceful, productive, and happy people. He also explains that Walden Two's decision-making system is not authoritarian, or even democratic. Except for a small fluctuating group of community organizers, called Planners, Walden Two has no real governing body. Each member of the community is apparently self-motivated, with the freedom to select a new place to work each day which supports the common good. Rather than money, the community uses a simple system of points that buys greater leisure periods in exchange for less desirable labour. Community members automatically receive ample food, and the extremely relaxed work schedule of only four hours of work a day on average leaves them with ample time to meet their higher needs by nurturing their creative, intellectual and sporting interests.

Perhaps most notably of all though, Walden Two does possess some more unusual customs. These include the expectation that children are raised communally, rather than by nuclear families, and that individuals follow the 'Walden Code' which is a set of guidelines for self-control techniques. The code encourages community members to credit all individual and other achievements to the larger community, and therefore personal expressions of thanks, for example, are taboo.

The novel is essentially a novel of ideas, in which the small number of characters debate and discuss the practicality, morality, and desirability of this utopian vision. During a number of private conversations, it is clear that Professor Burris is impressed by the successes of Walden Two but finds it difficult to look beyond Frazier's irritating pride and boastfulness about the community. Professor Castle, meanwhile, accuses Frazier of despotism, to which Frazier responds by asserting that Walden Two is a place safe from all forms of despotism, even the 'despotism of democracy'.

These ideas perhaps offer an insight into why Skinner's advocacy of cultural design provoked such condemnation in America. His ideas were viewed as un-American and flew in the face of the individualistic American dream, family values and democracy. The views of Professor Castle may represent those of mainstream America, whereby the design of Walden Two is likened to that used by dictators but not by men of good will.

Beyond Freedom and Dignity

The controversy of cultural design and what it meant for the freedom and dignity of the individual wasn't truly felt by mainstream America, however, until many years after the publication of *Walden Two*, when a different book – *Beyond Freedom and Dignity* – was published. Whether it was the book's provocative title, or the sensitivities of mainstream America during the Vietnam War era, it is hard to know exactly why it prompted such a furore. But it was a response that has been reserved for only very few intellectuals in recent history.

Beyond Freedom and Dignity does not contain any new findings, nor does it expound any new theories. What begins as a basic lesson in behavioural science and operant conditioning for the general reader soon expands into a grand visionary work, reflecting on how human beings and their culture have got to this point and what awaits us in the future. Freedom, Skinner says, is an illusion because no human beings are autonomous. Instead, our 'freedom' of choice depends entirely on our conditioning. As a result, dignity too becomes a questionable concept, as there can be no dignity in simply acting in a manner in which we have been conditioned to act. For Skinner, dignity is merely the absence of *visible* conditioning. We don't tend to give people as much credit for achievements where the causes of their behaviour (such as earning money or escaping from harm) are clear to see. We even try to gain credit by disguising or concealing the true causes of our behaviour. We insist that we didn't *have* to act in that way, even if the truth is that we did. Skinner's analysis rejects 'dignity' as a false notion of inner causality which removes both credit for action and blame for misdeeds. He insists that, as our scientific understanding of behaviour increases, 'the achievements for which a person himself is to be given credit seem to approach zero' (Skinner, 1971).

Skinner acknowledges that the concepts of freedom and dignity have led to many positive advances in the human condition, but that they may now be hindering the advance of a technology of human behaviour and cultural design. Faced with the possibility of extinction, as a result of climate change, overpopulation and war, our entrenched belief in individual freedom and dignity is preventing us from truly understanding how our behaviour is shaped through the contingencies of our human societies, and from seeing how we can change these contingencies to change our behaviour and eliminate these threats. Skinner argues that only a technology of behaviour will be able to create a culture in which optimal conditions exist.

Skinner concludes with an explanation of what the radical behaviourist philosophy means for the individual. Although it clearly assigns aspects of a person's character to environmental factors – aspects which they may consider to be driven by their own 'will' – Skinner is keen to stress that his analysis does not 'leave an empty organism' as 'man remains what he has always been'. The final sentence of the book frames the Skinnerian vision of the future as a positive one: 'A scientific view of man offers exciting possibilities. We have not yet seen what man can make of man.'

However, this is a vision that many in America could not tolerate. Vice president Spiro Agnew may have summed up this feeling when he said at the time: 'The "meaning of life" is seriously challenged by Skinner's ideas, the adoption of which would guarantee that life becomes devoid of meaning.' (Agnew in Rutherford, 2009)

Such a reaction came as no surprise to Skinner, who had acknowledged in his book, *Science and Human Behavior*, nearly 20 years earlier, that 'it has always been the unfortunate task of science to dispossess cherished beliefs regarding the place of man in the universe'. As Skinner saw it though, 'the highest human dignity may be to accept facts of human behaviour regardless of their momentary implications'.

The Strange Death of Radical Behaviourism

After Skinner's death in 1990, it was historian Thomas Leahey's book, *A History of Psychology* (1992), which first referred to radical behaviourism's 'strange death'. It was strange because, despite all of the obituaries written by many in the field of psychology and beyond, behaviour analysis was in fact in good health. Skinner had himself predicted that radical behaviourism would one day 'die', but from its success not failure. He knew that it would no longer be needed as a distinct philosophy because the issues that had shaped its formation, like the dismissal of mentalism and positivism, were resolved and its ideas had become part of mainstream psychology. The widespread take-up and application of Skinner's ideas even led the President of the Association for Psychological Science in 2004, Henry Roediger III, to state in his article titled 'What Happened to Behaviorism', that radical behaviourism had 'actually won the intellectual battle' and 'in a very real sense, all psychologists today (at least those doing empirical research) are [radical] behaviorists'.

Of course Skinner would take no credit for the ideas he proposed, nor would he claim that his perseverance in communicating these ideas in the face of strong criticism was in any way courageous. He himself had been shaped by the contingencies of his environment. In the same way rats had responded to the reinforcement of food in the Skinner Box, he had in turn been reinforced by their response and extinction rates, reinforcing his behaviour as scientist and philosopher. There was no freedom or dignity in his behaviour, he was merely an organism like any other, responding to his environment.

Conclusion

Today, every psychology student is taught that behaviourism in all its forms was displaced by the cognitive revolution, because it was deeply flawed scientifically. It is true that cognitive psychology, with its focus on the internal mental processes of thinking and memory amongst others, has flourished in the decades following Chomsky's infamous critique of Skinner's *Verbal Behavior*. Nonetheless, behaviour analysis hasn't been entirely replaced and, in some respects, has flourished as well. Indeed, it could be argued that Chomsky's review demonstrated a kind of naïve understanding of radical behaviourism that is evident in a great deal of psychology teaching today. That is, that Skinner was an extreme environmentalist, dogmatically prophesizing that all behaviour resulted from a stimulus–response mechanism, and that internal mental processes had no place or significance in psychology. Whether this misrepresentation of Skinner has been intentional or the result of misunderstanding Skinner's position is open to debate, but it may have led many to overlook radical behaviourism in favour of cognitive and biological approaches to psychological science.

Radical Behaviourism Today

Behaviour analysis has a long history of applying operant conditioning techniques to a variety of specialized settings. As well as the use of token economies in psychiatric institutions, prisons and special schools (covered in Chapter 4), it has also influenced the development of therapeutic techniques, such as Acceptance and Commitment Therapy (ACT) and Dialectical Behaviour Therapy (DBT), amongst others. Such techniques are still used to great effect to this day. Interestingly, in many of these settings the professionals involved are often unaware of the origins of these techniques, focusing instead on simply how helpful they are for their clients.

Outside of these specific contexts though, many would argue that modern psychology in the broader sense now favours cognitive and biological models of human behaviour, especially since the development of brain scanning techniques and the surge in interest in neuroscience. However, even here it is wrong to assume that radical behaviourism no longer plays a role. Although it is often suggested that Skinner ignored our inner biology, this is also inaccurate. As well as his consideration of the role played by evolution (or phylogeny) as covered in Chapter 5, Skinner was also quite explicit on this issue. In *About Behaviorism*, he stated: 'The organism is not empty, of course, and it cannot adequately be treated like a "black box".'

While he argued that we do not need to understand our internal biological functioning in order to study the effects of the external environment on behaviour, he also felt that although the two fields were exploring different issues, ultimately they could complement one another. Neuroscience, for example, has helped identify which parts of our brains are active when we perform specific functions. However, it cannot explain the meaning of our behaviour in its environmental context or why those functions are performed.

One modern field of research where ideas from both radical behaviourism and biology could complement each other is in that of epigenetics. This is the study of how changes in organisms are caused by the modification of the ways genes are expressed rather than alteration of the genes themselves. This can include the way that our interactions with the environment influence our genes which can, in turn, affect our behaviour.

In a study with echoes of behaviourist conditioning techniques, Dias and Ressler (2014) conditioned male mice to fear the smell of cherry blossom by exposing them to the odour while giving them a small electric shock to their feet. Eventually, the mice exhibited fear of the smell even when it was delivered without the accompanying shocks. After the mice had reproduced, the offspring of those mice went on to demonstrate the same fearful response despite never themselves having encountered the smell of cherry blossom. The offspring also had an increased number of cherry blossom smell receptors in their brain. Meanwhile, the offspring of mice that had been conditioned to fear another smell, or mice who'd had no such conditioning at all, both demonstrated no fear of cherry blossom. It was concluded that trauma experienced through the environment can be passed on in families via some sort of epigenetic mechanism.

The idea of inheriting learned experience is controversial, as scientific convention states that genes contained in DNA are the only way to transmit biological information between generations. However, the field of epigenetics has demonstrated that our genes are modified by the environment all the time. It is possible that chemical tags that attach themselves to our DNA might somehow be passed through generations, meaning our environment could have an impact on our children's health and behaviour. Research in humans has even suggested that the trauma suffered by Holocaust survivors is capable of being passed on to their children, the clearest sign yet that one person's life experience can affect subsequent generations (Yehuda et al, 1998).

Epigenetics has a long way to go in order to truly understand how environmental events might impact on the expression of our genes through the generations. However, behaviour analysis is a key partner in this research. Not only do both operate within the same evolutionary framework, but behaviour analysis has a long history of research – developed by Skinner and others – that is needed to understand our relationship with the environment. In this sense, radical behaviourism is alive and thriving, albeit within new and ever-evolving fields within modern psychological science.

Skinner's Legacy

What Skinner showed the scientific world, through his life and work, was a willingness to ask difficult questions and a boldness to have ambitions to change the world. It could be said that he was only ever controversial because other people were unwilling to question the values they hold most dear, regardless of what the scientific evidence might suggest. This unwillingness represents the very issue he was trying to address. Skinner confronted issues such as pollution and climate change and overpopulation long before it was fashionable to do so, framing these existential threats to humanity as issues, not for the sciences of biology or physics, but behavioural science. However, in a sense Skinner's harshest critics were right. They were keen to portray him as a purveyor of tools of manipulation to be used for increasing governmental control that would appeal to dictators in a totalitarian state. While Skinner never wanted his behavioural science to be used for anything of the sort, it may be that his critics were right about the control, but simply wrong about the controller.

In a modern world increasingly dominated by the Internet and 'Big Tech', it may be private industry rather than central government who have become the controllers. Online marketing and social media organizations have been quick to realize the profit-making potential in using reinforcement to shape human behaviour for their own restricted interests. Rather than pigeons pecking keys for reinforcement in the form of food, many of us have become disposed to checking our devices for reinforcement in the form of 'followers', 'likes', 'retweets', or 'levelling up' in online games. Every sort of firm, from social media giants to online gambling companies, have used schedules and contingencies of reinforcement to great effect, while Skinner's utopian dream remains a distant prospect. In an age of big data, GPS positioning, genetic mapping, and artificial intelligence, technology has the power to know us better than ever before. When this data is combined with operant conditioning techniques, technology has the power to motivate us to live healthier, less polluting, and more peaceful lives just as much as it can manipulate us for profit. A willingness to confront these issues head on may be what Skinner would want us to do.

Bibliography

Works by Skinner

Skinner, B. F. (1938) *The Behavior of Organisms: An experimental analysis*. New York: Appleton-Century.

Skinner, B. F. (1947) '"Superstition" in the pigeon'. *Journal of Experimental Psychology*, 38, pp. 168-172.

Skinner, B. F. (1948) *Walden Two*. New York: Macmillan.

Skinner, B. F. (1953) *Science and Human Behavior*. New York: Macmillan.

Skinner, B. F. and Ferster, C. B. (1957) *Schedules of Reinforcement*. New York: Appleton-Century-Crofts.

Skinner, B. F. (1957) *Verbal Behavior*. New York: Appleton-Century-Crofts.

Skinner, B. F. (1966) 'The Phylogeny and Ontogeny of Behavior'. *Science*, 153, pp. 1205-13.

Skinner, B. F. (1968) *The Technology of Teaching*. New York: Appleton-Century-Crofts.

Skinner, B. F. (1969) *Contingencies of Reinforcement: A theoretical analysis*. New York: Appleton-Century-Crofts.

Skinner, B. F. (1971) *Beyond Freedom and Dignity*. New York: Knopf.

Skinner, B. F. (1974) *About Behaviorism*. New York: Knopf.

Skinner, B. F. (1976) *Particulars of My Life*. New York: Knopf.

Skinner, B. F. (1979) *The Shaping of a Behaviorist: Part Two of an Autobiography*. New York: Knopf.

Skinner, B. F., Epstein, R., and Lanza, R. P. (1980) 'Symbolic Communication between Two Pigeons'. (Columba livia domestics). *Science*, 1980, 207, pp. 543-45.

Other works cited

Breland, K. and Breland, M. (1961) 'The Misbehavior of Organisms'. *American Psychologist*, 16, 681.

Bjork, D.W. (1993) *B.F. Skinner, A Life*. New York: Basic Books.

Chomsky, A. Noam (1959) 'A Review of Skinner's Verbal Behavior'. *Language*, 35 (1).

Dias, B. G. and Ressler, K. J. (2013) 'Parental olfactory experience influences behavior and neural structure in subsequent generations'. *Nature Neuroscience*, 17, pp. 89–96.

Dews, P. B. (1970) *Festschrift for B. F. Skinner*. New York: Irvington.

Donahoe J.W. (1984) 'Skinner – The Darwin of Ontogeny?' *Behavioral and Brain Sciences*, 7(4), pp. 487–488.

Leahey, T.H. (1992) *A History of Psychology* (3rd edition). Englewood Cliffs, NJ: Prentice-Hall.

Los Angeles Times (1990) 'Psychologist Skinner Dies of Leukemia'. Retrieved 15 November 2019 from https://www.latimes.com/archives/la-xpm-1990-08-20-mn-780-story.html.

Haggbloom, S. J., Warnick, R., Warnick, J. E., Jones, V. K., Yarbrough, G. L., Russell, T. M., Borecky, C. M., McGahhey, R., Powell, J. L., Beavers, J., Monte, E. (2002) 'The 100 most eminent psychologists of the 20th century'. *Review of General Psychology*, 6, pp. 139–152.

Roediger, H.L (2004) 'What Happened to Behaviorism?' *Observer*, 17(3). Retrieved 10 November 2019 from https://www.psychologicalscience.org/observer/what-happened-to-behaviorism.

Romanes, G. J. (1892) *Animal intelligence*. London: Kegan Paul Trench & Co.

Rutherford, A. (2009) *Beyond the Box: B.F. Skinner's technology of behavior from laboratory to life, 1950s–1970s*. Toronto: University of Toronto Press.

Schwartz, S. (1986) *Classic Studies in Psychology*. Palo Alto: Mayfield Publishing.

Vargas, J.S. (n.d.). 'Brief biography of B.F. Skinner'. Retrieved from website of *B.F. Skinner Foundation* January 15, 2020 at: https://www.bfskinner.org/archives/biographical-information/.

Watson, J. B. (1913) 'Psychology as the Behaviorist Views It'. *Psychological Review*, 20, pp. 158-177.

Watson, J.B. (1925) *Behaviorism*. New York: Norton.

Watson, J. B. and Rayner, R. (1920) 'Conditioned Emotional Reactions'. *Journal of Experimental Psychology*, 3, pp. 1-14.

Watson, J.B. and Rayner, R. (1928) *The Psychological Care of Infant and Child*. New York: Norton.

Yehuda, R., Schmeidler, J., Wainberg, M., Binder-Brynes, K., and Duvdevani, T. (1998) 'Vulnerability to posttraumatic stress disorder in adult offspring of Holocaust survivors'. *American Journal of Psychiatry* 155: pp. 1163–1171.

Biography

Tom Buxton-Cope graduated in Psychology from Manchester University, UK, and went on to complete an MA in Education, qualifying to be a teacher. He has taught psychology for over 10 years, and has held the position of Head of Psychology in various educational establishments. He is also an A-level (college-level) examiner. He writes regular Psychology Factsheets for Curriculum Press and has authored several articles in *Psychology Review* for Hodder Education. Tom currently lives in Stockport, Greater Manchester, UK.

Acknowledgements

I'd like to thank Alice Bowden at Bowden & Brazil for giving me the opportunity to write this book, and to Sarah Tomley for her clear guidance, too. I would also like to thank my family for their support and patience throughout the period of researching and writing this book, particularly my wife for tolerating the pile of papers and books on the dining room table.

Picture Credits

Fig. 1 'Miss Graves', B.F. Skinner Foundation. Fig. 2 'Skinner aged 19', B.F. Skinner Foundation. Fig. 3 'Skinner with Yvonne', B.F. Skinner Foundation. Fig. 4 'Ivan Pavlov', Unknown author (https://commons.wikimedia.org/wiki/File:Ivan_Pavlov_1934.jpg), https://creativecommons.org/licenses/by/4.0/legalcode. Fig. 5 'Skinner with his friend, Keller, 1931', B.F. Skinner Foundation. Fig. 6 'Skinner Box', V1nzorg (https://commons.wikimedia.org/wiki/File:Skinner_box_de.png), „Skinner box de", text, https://creativecommons.org/licenses/by-sa/3.0/legalcode. Fig. 7 'Example of operant conditioning using a pigeon as the test subject', Mark E. Bouton from University of Vermont (https://commons.wikimedia.org/wiki/File:Operant_Conditioning_Involves_Choice.png), https://creativecommons.org/licenses/by-sa/4.0/legalcode. Fig. 8 'A pigeon is guided into a glide missile, as part of Skinner's Project Pigeon, 1943', B.F. Skinner Foundation. Fig. 9 'Skinner's daughter Deborah in the baby tender, or 'aircrib', 1944', B.F. Skinner Foundation. Fig. 10 'An example of one of Skinner's teaching machines', Silly rabbit (https://commons.wikimedia.org/wiki/File:Skinner_teaching_machine_08.jpg), „Skinner teaching machine 08", https://creativecommons.org/licenses/by/3.0/legalcode

www.ingramcontent.com/pod-product-compliance
Ingram Content Group UK Ltd.
Pitfield, Milton Keynes, MK11 3LW, UK
UKHW041640190726
13854UKWH00006B/2616

9 781999 949280